COMMUNICATION SKILLS FOR ADULTS

Your No-BS Guide to Being Heard, Setting Boundaries, Speaking with Confidence and Spotting Lies

Tali Moss

Dedicated to

The overthinkers, the people-pleasers, the silent simmerers, and anyone who's ever walked away from a conversation replaying what they should have said instead.

This one's for you.

So you can stop second-guessing,

start being heard,

and finally take up the space you were always **meant to own.**

CONTENTS

INTRODUCTION:
Communication is Your Secret Weapon
(Don't Screw It Up)

This is not your average "how to talk good" book.

You won't find robotic scripts, cheesy affirmations, or recycled TED Talk advice here.

And if you're hoping for a lecture from someone who's never survived a tense Zoom call or defused a 3am "we need to talk" text—keep it moving.

But...

If you're tired of being misunderstood, tired of getting talked over, tired of watching mediocre loudmouths win just because they know how to work a room—then grab a drink, silence your notifications, and keep reading.

Because *this* is the communication guide for people who are done playing small.

What This Book WILL Do for You

✓ **Turn you into the person everyone wants to talk to.** Not because you say the most, but because you *listen* better than anyone else in the room.

✓ **Help you cut through the noise.** Whether it's dealing with office politics, navigating relationships, or commanding attention in a crowded space, you'll learn how to communicate with impact.

✓ **Give you real-world, no-BS strategies.** No jargon, no fluff, just sharp, tactical ways to get people to actually listen when you speak.

✓ **Teach you how to spot lies, manipulation, and deception.** Because let's face it—being able to call out bullshit (without causing a scene) is an elite-level life skill. ✓ **Make you feel in control of every conversation.** No more awkward stammering, over-explaining, or getting talked over like you're a background extra in your own life.

What This Book WON'T Do for You

✖ **Give you a personality transplant.** You don't need to become a loud, fake extrovert to be a great communicator. You just need to master the right tools.

✖ **Teach you how to "win" every conversation.** This isn't about overpowering people—it's about learning how to *connect* and *influence* without being a jerk.

✖ **Waste your time with outdated advice.** You won't find any "just be yourself" clichés here. The world has changed, and so has the way we communicate.

✖ **Turn you into a mind reader.** But you *will* learn how to read between the lines, decode hidden signals, and tell when someone's lying through their teeth.

Why This Matters (And Why You Need to Read Every Page)

Most people go through life **thinking** they're great communicators, but in reality? They're just talking at people, hoping something sticks. **That's why they struggle.**

The people who thrive—at work, in relationships, in everyday life—aren't always the smartest, the funniest, or the most charismatic. **They're the ones who know how to listen, how to read the room, and how to make every word count.**

This book is going to teach you how to do exactly that. So, buckle up. **By the time you finish this book, you won't just be better at communicating—you'll be unstoppable.**

⚠️ Heads-up: Emoji Alert

This book covers *digital* communication too—texts, chats, DMs, and all the emoji-laced chaos that comes with it. That means you'll see a lot of emojis used as examples. Some may not print perfectly depending on your device or paperback formatting, but they're included on purpose. It's 2025—we don't just speak in words anymore.

CHAPTER 1:

Say What You Mean (Without Sounding Like a Jerk)

Clarity is kindness. Vagueness?
That's just how you piss people off in slow motion.

The Real Problem—You're Not Being Heard, You're Being Decoded

Most of us think we're being clear when we speak. We do. We believe we're laying things out in a normal, reasonable way. We explain. We gesture. We throw in a "Does that make sense?" like a polite little punctuation mark. And then we're absolutely stunned when someone stares back at us, confused, defensive, or (worse) totally unaffected—like they just listened to a weather report and not, you know, our *actual point.*

Lo and behold… they didn't hear a word of what you said. They heard what they **think** you meant.

And that gap? **That's where everything falls apart.** Misunderstandings, missed promotions, fights that make you question your sanity—none of it starts with what you said. It starts with how it was received. Or decoded. Or (in some cases) completely misinterpreted by someone who read the tone wrong, filled in the blanks, and assumed the worst. And then made it your fault.

It's maddening. Especially when you walk away from a conversation thinking, *Wait, how did they get THAT from what I said?*

So, let's zoom out. The issue isn't just that people misunderstand you. It's that most of us are out here communicating like we're on a first date with every sentence. We're trying to be interesting, likeable, non-threatening, articulate, professional, emotionally fluent, concise, humble, and warm—*all at once.* And in that attempt to be all things to all people, we end up being… vague. Passive. Awkward. Or worse: forgettable.

You say something with heart and urgency—something you **need** them to get, and it lands like a polite email from HR. They skim it. They mentally check out. They say, "Got it," when they absolutely didn't. And then they do the opposite of what you hoped for, and you're left wondering if you're just speaking in a dialect no one told you about.

That's not your imagination. That's the **decode gap**—the space between your intention and their interpretation.

And you know what: **it's usually filled with their assumptions, not your meaning.**

They're not hearing your careful phrasing. They're scanning for tone, looking for subtext, playing their own mental Mad Libs with your words. And if your delivery leaves room for doubt, they'll fill it with whatever insecurity, suspicion, or distraction they brought into the conversation that day. Which means your message? It's not being heard the way you said it. It's being filtered through someone else's chaos.

So, what do we do?

We try to compensate. We explain more. We soften the edges. We rephrase mid-sentence. We check their face for clues. We trail off when they blink too slowly. We turn direct thoughts into nervous TED Talks, hoping that if we talk long enough and nicely enough, they'll finally *get it.*

And in the process, we forget the one thing that actually makes people listen: **CLARITY**. Not perfection. Not politeness. Not volume. Just... clarity. Unapologetic, deliberate, human clarity.

But that feels risky, right? Because clarity often looks like saying something directly. And saying something directly feels a bit like stepping off a cliff with no people-pleasing parachute. You worry you'll sound rude, or cold, or too blunt. You worry they'll take it the wrong way, that they'll think you're bossy or aggressive or—God forbid—confident. So, you wrap your message in disclaimers and diffusers and 27 hundred unnecessary words.

And guess what? It doesn't help. It just buries your point in bubble wrap.

Because the truth is: **if your message needs a decoder ring, you've already lost the room.**

People are busy. People are tired. People don't have the mental bandwidth to dig through your verbal packaging looking for what you *actually* meant to say. They'll decide what they think you meant based on how it *felt*, and how much room you left for interpretation. And if what you said felt vague, hesitant, or emotionally confusing? That's on you. Even if your heart was in the right place.

So, before we go anywhere else in this book, you need to know this:

Being clear is not the same as being rude.

Being direct is not the same as being cold.

And saying what you mean does not make you a jerk.

It makes you someone who's finally worth listening to.

Why You Over-Explain (And What It's Costing You)

Let's not pretend this is just a communication issue. Over-explaining isn't just about being "wordy" or "long-winded"—it's about **fear**. Specifically, the fear of being misunderstood, disliked, dismissed, or judged for having a thought that lands too hard without enough soft padding.

So, we pad.

We pad everything. We soften. We explain before we say the thing. Then we say the thing. Then we explain why we said it. And just in case that wasn't enough, we add a "does that make sense?" at the end like a sad little garnish.

Because deep down, we're not just trying to be clear. We're trying to protect ourselves.

From what? From the look on someone's face that says "Wow, that was direct." From the possibility that they'll take it the wrong way. From being perceived as too assertive. Or not friendly enough. Or cold. Or intimidating. Or difficult. Or—God help us—*confident and female at the same time.*

So, we over-explain.

We give five reasons where one would do. We say "I just wanted to quickly say" before saying something that isn't quick or "just."

We throw in unnecessary disclaimers like, "Maybe I'm wrong, but…" even when we're not wrong and we know it.

We flood the space with words hoping it will soften the edge of whatever truth we're trying to say.

And sometimes, we don't even realize we're doing it. We think we're being helpful. Polite. Thoughtful. Considerate. But really, we're watering ourselves down to make our presence easier to swallow.

And then we wonder why no one really listens.

But here's the brutal truth most people won't tell you:

Over-explaining makes you sound unsure—even when you're not.

Even when you're right. Even when your instincts are spot on. If you deliver them wrapped in bubble wrap and 800 qualifiers, people won't take them seriously. Because they'll assume that *you* don't.

This is the part that's hard to admit.

Because on the surface, over-explaining looks like you're just being thorough. But underneath, it's self-protection. It's a subconscious attempt to preempt any discomfort the other person might feel by making yourself smaller. Less threatening. More "digestible."

You think you're helping. But what you're really doing is **giving people room to doubt you.**

And they will.

They'll assume you're not sure of what you're saying. They'll talk over you, rephrase your idea louder, or nod politely and then do the exact opposite of what you suggested. Not because you were wrong. But because you said it like a question. Because you delivered your clarity in a way that made it easy to ignore.

So, if you've ever felt invisible in meetings, or like your feedback doesn't land, or like people always listen to the louder, more confident-sounding (but not smarter) person—this is probably why. It's not that they're more right. It's that they don't sound like they're asking permission to exist.

And I know, I know—you've been told your whole life to be nice. To be polite. To explain yourself. Especially if you're in any role, job, or gender where being *too* direct was framed as "not a good look."

But here's the thing:

Politeness doesn't require a 12-paragraph preamble. Respect doesn't mean diluting your message into emotional soup.

Kindness doesn't mean shrinking.

You can be direct *and* kind. You can be clear *and* compassionate. You can say, "No, I don't agree with that," or "Here's what I think would work better," without being a monster. But you'll never get there if you're still trying to be invisible while hoping people notice you.

So, here's your first real challenge: **watch yourself.**

The next time you're in a conversation and you feel the urge to explain something for the third time—or start your sentence with "I could be wrong, but…"—stop. Just for a second.

Ask yourself:

- Am I adding clarity, or just softening the impact?
- Am I being thoughtful, or just afraid to be misread?
- Am I owning what I'm saying, or am I trying to get a hall pass for having an opinion?

Because yes, it might feel safer to be vague. **But vagueness doesn't build trust. Clarity does.** And clarity without apology? That's the foundation of respect.

And that's where you start getting taken seriously.

The Weak Language Trap

This one's going to sting a little. Because we all do it. Every one of us. The "justs," the "I thinks," the "maybe it's just me but"—these aren't harmless little conversational flourishes. They're *camouflage.* They're what you say when you don't want to fully commit to your words, just in case someone raises an eyebrow or doesn't like what you said.

And they are draining your authority faster than a group text with three Karens and one unmuted iPhone mic.

Let's start with the classics.

"I'm just wondering…"

No, you're not *just* wondering. You have a thought, a question, a concern. But you're trying to make it sound breezy and non-threatening, like you're gently knocking on the door instead of walking in with a point.

"I could be wrong, but…"

You probably *aren't* wrong. You probably know exactly what you're talking about. But that sentence tells the room you're already bracing for impact.

"Does that make sense?"

Said after every clear, coherent statement as if you just spoke in Morse code and need someone to confirm you didn't black out in the middle of a sentence.

"Sorry, I just…"

If you're genuinely apologizing, fine. But nine times out of ten, this is a preemptive apology for taking up space. You're not sorry. You're trying to seem softer so no one thinks you're "too much."

And look, we've all been conditioned to speak this way. Especially if you've ever been told you're intimidating, opinionated, difficult, "too direct," "too emotional," or the dreaded "abrasive." Somewhere along the way, you started padding everything you said to seem more agreeable. More digestible. Less threatening.

But language is power. And if the language you're using is constantly undercutting your own thoughts, don't be surprised when no one listens the first time.

Weak language doesn't make you sound polite. It makes you sound unsure.

It creates this invisible little asterisk next to everything you say. Like you're putting disclaimers on your own opinions before anyone else has a chance to disagree.

And here's the part that hurts: it's not helping. Not even a little. It's not making people like you more. It's not making them respect your perspective. It's making them ignore you. Or interrupt you. Or smile politely and then rephrase what you just said with more confidence—so *they* get the credit for your idea.

Yes, it's infuriating. But it's also fixable.

Start small. Pick one weak phrase, just one—that you notice yourself using. "I think." "Maybe." "I'm sorry, but…" **Catch it. Pause. Replace it with nothing.** Literally, just remove the filler and say the damn thing.

Don't "think we might need a different approach." Say, "We need a different approach."

Don't "just want to quickly say." Say, "Here's what I want to add."

You don't need to be rude. You don't need to talk like a drill sergeant or bark orders or pretend to be some alpha extrovert who thrives on confrontation. You just need to sound like you actually **mean** what you're saying.

Because if you don't back your own words, who will?

Confidence doesn't always come from volume. It comes from economy. From knowing what you want to say, and saying it cleanly, without all the anxious emotional packaging. And no, it won't always be comfortable. At first, it'll feel exposed. A little naked. You'll say something short and direct and your brain will immediately scream "Add more words! Fill the silence!"

Don't.

Let your point land. Let it breathe. Watch how people sit up when you speak, because there's nothing confusing about it anymore.

This is your first real upgrade. Stop giving people reasons not to take you seriously.

Stop shrinking your sentences to make your presence feel smaller.

Say what you mean. Then stop talking.

How to Speak Clearly Without Sounding Like a Tool

Here's where a lot of people get tripped up: they finally muster the courage to speak clearly, and then someone calls them "rude," "too blunt," or the all-time favorite—"intense." And suddenly they're spiraling back into the land of qualifiers and emotional disclaimers because the last thing they want is to sound like a corporate memo with anger issues.

But direct doesn't equal jerk.

Being clear isn't about tone-policing yourself into robot mode or tearing through people with blunt force. It's about owning your message, without apology, and without ego. Think: calm. Grounded. Zero drama. You can be kind and still speak with backbone.

Here's how to do it.

---

1. Ditch the runway. Just take off.

You don't need to warm people up with, "Sorry to bother you, I just wanted to quickly touch base…"

No. You're not interrupting a hostage negotiation. You're asking a question or stating a need.

Instead of: "Sorry, I know you're super busy, but I was just wondering if maybe…"

Try: "Can I check something with you?" or "I need a quick decision on this."

It's not cold. It's clear.

---

2. Speak in statements, not apologies.

If you're always asking for permission to speak—verbally or energetically—you're making your voice optional. Say what you mean like you expect to be heard. Not tolerated.

Instead of: "I might be wrong but I think we should maybe…"

Try: "Here's what I think would work better."

You're not steamrolling anyone. You're just making it easier for them to actually *hear* you without sifting through 16 layers of maybe.

---

3. Keep your tone warm, not wobbly.

People confuse "kind" with "vague," and "clear" with "aggressive." But the magic is in the *energy* you bring—not the length of your sentence. Short doesn't mean sharp. It just means you're not wasting their time or your own.

You can say:

"I don't think that's the right fit."

…with a steady voice, a neutral face, and a tone that says *I'm grounded, not attacking you.*

Clarity plus calm = respect.

---

4. Use anchoring phrases.

If you're nervous about how something might land, use phrases that give context *without* backpedaling.

Try these:

- "From what I've seen…"
- "Here's what I'm noticing…"
- "The way I'm reading this is…"
- "I want to be direct about something."

These let people know you're not being reactive—you're being intentional. It keeps the conversation human, not robotic.

---

5. Let your sentences land.

This one's huge. Once you've said what you needed to say—*stop talking.* Don't ramble. Don't fill the silence. Don't soften it with a "But that's just my two cents!" smile.

Let it land. Give it space.

Silence is not your enemy. It's where impact sinks in.

---

6. When in doubt, mirror how you'd want to be spoken to.

Think about the people you admire—the ones who speak and people lean in. Are they vague? Over-explaining? Constantly padding every sentence with emotional cushioning? No.

They're kind. But they're **solid**.

They use plain language.

They own their words.

They make it easy for you to understand what they're saying, and how they feel about it.

Do the same. People will feel it.

This isn't about bulldozing your way through conversations or turning into a professional boundary-setting machine. It's about speaking with **integrity**, not insecurity. About replacing nervous air quotes with clean language that leaves no room for confusion.

Clarity is a kindness.

And you're allowed to say what you mean without making yourself small first.

Try This — The 30-Second Test

Here's the rule of thumb you must remember: **if you can't say it clearly in 30 seconds, you probably don't know what you're trying to say yet.**

That's not a dig—it's a diagnosis. Most of us don't speak too much because we're want to be heard. We speak too much because we're **unclear**. We ramble when we're working out our point out loud, hoping the other person will hang in there long enough for us to figure out what the hell we meant by the time we reach the end of the sentence.

But clarity doesn't show up at the end. It's there from the first word. And when it's not, people check out. Or tune in just long enough to misinterpret you.

So, here's a tool you can actually use. It's simple. It's uncomfortable. And it works.

The 30-Second Test

Take anything you want to say—something important, something sticky, something that matters, and try to say it in 30 seconds or less. No disclaimers. No fluff. No repeating yourself five different ways because you're afraid they won't get it the first time.

Just one clean, human, unfiltered statement of your point.

Try this:

- Explain what's bothering you at work in 30 seconds.

- Ask for what you need in a relationship in 30 seconds.
- Share a boundary without the 12-sentence justification.

You'll feel the urge to expand. You'll want to soften the edges. You'll think you *need* to add "just" or "maybe" or "sorry, I'm not great at explaining this."

Resist it.

Clarity is what you say when you stop performing and start respecting your own time.

And no, this doesn't mean you need to talk in headlines or bark orders like some personal-growth bro on a podcast. It just means being intentional. Cutting the noise. Giving your words a backbone.

Here's the magic part: if you can say it in 30 seconds, you can say it in a way people actually remember.

Because guess what they remember? Not your perfectly crafted phrasing. Not your five-point supporting argument. They remember how it felt to listen to you. Was it sharp or messy? Clean or cluttered? Did it land or did it dribble out over three minutes of self-doubt?

The 30-Second Test forces you to get clear before you open your mouth. It makes you think *before* you speak, which is radical in a world where most people are just waiting for their turn to talk.

So, the next time you feel that anxious tangle in your chest, like you *know* what you want to say but you're already bracing for how it might land—pause. Run it through the 30-Second Test.

You'll stumble at first. You'll over-explain and catch yourself halfway through. Good. That's how you learn. That's how you clean up your communication hygiene.

Because once you stop explaining the same point five ways and start saying it once, clearly and with intention?

People start listening.

They start respecting.

And more importantly—they start *getting it.*

So, here's where we land: You don't need to become louder. You don't need to grow a fake backbone or rehearse a new personality. You just need to **stop shrinking your message to make people comfortable**. Clear is kind. Direct is generous. And speaking like you mean it isn't rude—it's respect, both for yourself and the person you're talking to. You're allowed to say what you mean. Now let's work on making sure people actually hear it.

CHAPTER 2:

Shut Up and Listen

(Seriously, Just Shut Up)

Most people listen to reply, not to understand, which is why they suck at it.

Listening Is a Power Move, Not a Passive One

Listening is not what happens when your mouth is shut and you're silently plotting your next brilliant point. It's not passive, it's not submissive, and it sure as hell isn't weakness. Listening—the kind that actually lands, connects, and influences—is one of the most commanding, underrated power moves in the human skill set. And yet, most people treat it like a background task, like waiting in line at the pharmacy. Just sit there. Nod. Try not to die of boredom. Smile vaguely while your brain scrolls through your mental to-do list.

No.

That's not listening. That's presence cosplay.

Real listening is active. It's disruptive. It demands restraint, control, and emotional intelligence. It's not sitting quietly like a beige conference room chair. It's intentionally choosing to *not* make everything about you—*especially* when the spotlight is there for the taking. That kind of self-restraint? That's power.

You know, most people think the person doing the most talking is the one in control. The loudest voice, the strongest opinion, the first to interrupt—*that's* who's winning the conversation, right?

Wrong.

And guess who's actually running the room? The person who's not interrupting, not scrambling to be heard, not bulldozing their way through a discussion like a human leaf blower. The person who's so grounded they don't need to be the center of attention to influence the direction of everything being said. They're not just hearing words—they're catching tone, context, what's *not* being said. And they're smart enough to know that when you actually listen, people *show you who they are.*

You want emotional intel? Listen.

You want leverage in a negotiation? Listen.

You want to know if your friend is spiraling or just having a bad day? Listen.

Because **people will always give themselves away**—verbally, emotionally, energetically—if you give them enough quiet to do it.

But here's the problem: we're wired to associate talking with value. "Add to the conversation," "Have your say," "Speak up," "Don't let them talk over you"—this stuff is baked into how we're taught to communicate from childhood. Silence, on the other hand, is painted as awkward, uncomfortable, weak. So, when we think of a "good communicator," we picture someone articulate, charismatic, who dominates a room with presence.

But **domination isn't the same as influence**. And charisma without awareness is just noise with good lighting.

So, let's flip the script. Let's rebrand listening from passive wallflower energy to what it actually is: **next-level leadership.**

Think about the people you trust the most. The ones you go to when your life is a chaotic dumpster fire of feelings and bad decisions. Are they the ones who immediately talk over you? Who hijack your story to insert their own? Who speed-run you to a solution like you're some broken appliance to be repaired?

No.

They're the ones who sit in the mess with you. Who nod at the right moments. Who ask questions that make you think, not flinch. Who say things like, "That makes sense," and "Tell me more." People who don't rush to fix it because they know the value isn't always in the fixing—it's in the *holding*. That's real power. Quiet power. Still power.

Listening says: I'm not here to dominate. I'm here to ***understand***.

It says: I'm not reacting. I'm reading. I'm observing. I'm gathering data.

It says: You matter enough for me to pause my ego and pay attention.

That lands. That changes people. That builds trust, and **trust is currency**. Especially in workplaces, relationships, and high-stakes moments where one wrong word can shut someone down for good.

Now, let's address the elephant in your inner monologue: "Okay, sure, but what if *I* have something important to say?"

You do. And you'll say it better if you've actually listened first.

When you listen—really listen—you know how to respond in a way that hits. You're not shooting in the dark, hoping your point lands. You're tailoring your message to the person in front of you, using their language, their context, their emotional cues. That's not people-pleasing. That's **strategic communication**.

Powerful listening isn't about silence. It's about ***awareness***.

The pause isn't a void—it's a tool. The stillness isn't submissive—it's intentional.

And yes, it's hard. It's hard to shut up when someone says something you disagree with. It's hard to not jump in when you think your story is better, or funnier, or more helpful. It's hard to stay curious when someone is annoying you, or triggering you, or going off about something you think is petty.

But that's the difference between listening and performing patience.

One is active. The other is a lie with good manners.

And people can tell the difference.

They can feel it when you're just waiting for your turn to talk. They can feel it when you're nodding to be polite but your eyes are darting like a squirrel on espresso. They can feel when your "uh huh" means "please hurry up." You think you're hiding it, but your whole nervous system is screaming "checked out."

So, now I'm asking you: next time you're in a conversation that matters, try doing less. Not because you don't have value to add, but because sometimes ***the most valuable thing you can do is shut the hell up and let the other person breathe.*** Let them unravel. Let them speak long enough to go past the rehearsed answer and into something real.

Because if you give people enough room to talk, they will always show you something you weren't expecting—about themselves, about the situation, sometimes even about you.

And if you're really listening? You'll catch it.

That's power. And it doesn't make a sound.

The Art of the Intentional Pause

Let's talk about the pause. The dreaded, awkward, skin-crawling pause. The silence that creeps into conversations like an uninvited guest and makes everyone want to sprint for the nearest topic change, apology, or distraction.

You know the one.

It shows up right after someone says something big—something heavy or vulnerable or not-that-funny, but nobody quite knows what to say next. So, what do we do? We panic. We fill it. We lunge for a reaction, a response, a witty comment, a safe detour—*anything* to avoid the terrible feeling that nothing is happening.

But here's the thing: *that* moment, that exact silence you're so desperate to escape from? That's where the good stuff lives. That's where truth starts to breathe. And if you can learn to sit in it, just sit and not flinch—you'll get access to things most people miss because they're too busy scrambling for noise.

The pause is not empty. It's information-rich.

It tells you whether someone is really done speaking, or just trying to find the courage to say the next part. It tells you whether they're being surface-level or if something deeper is trying to rise but keeps getting drowned out by your helpful chatter. It tells you if *you're* uncomfortable… or if they are.

Most people can't handle it. Silence makes them sweat. And not in a sexy, mysterious, power-move kind of way—more like "I need to make a joke or I'll explode" kind of way.

But when you can learn to hold a pause without freaking out? You unlock a totally different level of presence.

Because here's what happens when you *don't* fill the space:

- People keep talking.
- They go deeper.
- They reveal more than they meant to.
- They say the thing they didn't plan to say.
- And they trust you more for letting them get there.

It's not manipulation. It's permission. Permission for people to go past the polished, automatic surface-level stuff and actually process out loud. That doesn't happen when you're rushing in with advice or interrupting them with your version of the story or even just nodding too hard and saying "yeah, totally!" every six seconds. That's not support. That's panic in a socially acceptable disguise.

Here's a brutal truth: most people aren't actually listening. They're reacting. And silence short-circuits the reaction loop. It forces you to *feel* instead of *perform.* It creates space for emotional clarity, even when the words are clumsy or incomplete or painful. Especially then.

And yeah, sitting with that can be *really* uncomfortable.

You might feel awkward. You might feel exposed. You might feel like you're losing your grip on the conversation because the rhythm isn't flowing and your brain is screaming, *"Fix it! Save it! Rescue the vibe!"*

Don't.

Let it suck for a second.

Let the silence sit like a stone in the middle of the conversation. Let it thud. Let it echo. Let it stretch a little longer than feels polite. Let it hang there while both of you realize that something real might be coming next.

Because that discomfort? That's not failure. That's depth knocking.

And while we're here—can we talk about how *comically* bad most people are at this over text or DMs?

Someone sends you a vulnerable paragraph, and you respond in under ten seconds with "Oh no 😞 hope you're okay!" and then a meme. You didn't respond. You evacuated.

Silence in digital spaces is even harder because it feels like you're being rude or ghosting. But you're not. You're giving them (and yourself) time to read it twice. To absorb what's actually being said. To not just knee-jerk your way into the most emotionally performative response you can type.

Next time you get a message that hits heavy? Try this:

Don't reply right away. Not because you don't care, but because you do. And you're actually *reading* it. *Sitting* with it. *Choosing* your words like they matter. Because they do.

And if the silence feels too long? You can always send a quick "Reading. Brb. Want to give this the thought it deserves." That alone will already make you stand out in a world of rushed replies and robotic empathy.

Back to verbal convos—here's a simple challenge to start rewiring your impulse to fill silence:

Next time someone stops talking, count "one-one-thousand, two-one-thousand" in your head before responding.

That's two seconds. Feels like forever. But it's just long enough for you to make sure they're done, for them to decide if they want to say more, and for you to not blurt something out of pure social anxiety.

That pause? That's where your power is.

Because anyone can talk fast and dominate a room. But it takes serious emotional strength to sit in silence and let the moment unfold.

And no, that doesn't mean becoming a mute sage who just stares at people like a dramatic podcast host waiting for their viral quote. This isn't about being *weird.* It's about being *intentional.* It's about choosing your moments instead of reacting to every beat of a conversation like you're a contestant in a game show.

In fast-paced, performative culture, quiet is rebellion.

In emotionally reactive culture, quiet is maturity.

In relationships that matter, quiet is trust.

So, start practicing the pause. Let it stretch. Let it breathe. Let it do the work you keep trying to do with all your talking.

You don't need to fill the space. You *are* the space.

Mastering the Nonverbal Hell Yes

You can say all the right things, rehearse every line, pick just the right emoji combo, and still somehow make someone feel like they're talking to a brick wall—because the words are only part of the message. The rest? It's in your face, your body, your energy, your micro-reactions, your posture, your blink rate, your sighs, your fidgeting, your pacing, your way of leaning in or zoning out or raising an eyebrow when something doesn't sit right with you, and yes, even your silence. Especially your silence.

The brutal truth is, **you don't get to decide what people take away from you.** You don't get to declare yourself a great listener or a thoughtful friend or an emotionally available human being just because you *meant well.* You get measured by **how you make people feel** when they're around you—when they speak to you, when they open up to you, when they risk being a little bit more real than they usually allow themselves to be. And if your body language is sending "I'm bored," "I already know what you're going to say," or "I'd rather be anywhere else," then it doesn't matter how perfectly you've worded your "I totally get it" response. You don't get credit for being present when your presence is only technical.

Nonverbal listening is the part nobody teaches. Nobody pulls you aside in high school and says, "Hey, the way you cross your arms and stare at the wall during group work makes everyone feel like you hate them." Nobody breaks down how a sarcastic smirk when someone's being vulnerable can cut deeper than anything actually spoken. Believe me! It cuts like serrated knife straight to your liver!!

And yet, these are the signals people are *constantly* picking up on. Unconsciously. Automatically. Unforgivingly.

Because **most of us don't listen with our ears**—we listen with our *gut.* We're clocking cues we can't even articulate. We feel safe or exposed, welcomed or dismissed, not because someone said the magic words, but because something in their face or their energy told us we were either welcome to keep going—or subtly invited to shut the hell up.

So, if you want to become the kind of person people naturally open up to, the kind of person people trust, the kind of person whose presence alone puts others at ease—you've got to master the nonverbal *hell yes.*

What's that? It's the physical equivalent of "I'm here with you." It's the embodied, real-time signal that says, "I'm listening—not just waiting." It's the way your body supports the conversation, without stealing it.

It's **eye contact** that holds, without burning a hole in someone's soul. It's a **face** that responds in real-time—micro-nods, softening, raised brows, maybe even a quick inhale when something hits hard. It's s**houlders** that lean in slightly—not aggressively, but just enough to say, "I'm not trying to back away from your truth." It's **posture** that says "engaged" rather than "bored but too polite to bail." It's not faking interest—it's removing the distractions that keep you from actually being interested.

Let's get really specific. If you're constantly checking your phone, fiddling with your shirt, scanning the room, or adjusting your smartwatch like it's whispering state secrets into your wrist, *you are not listening.* You're sending a clear message: "I care, but only in the small gap between dopamine hits." And people feel that. They won't always call it out, but they'll file it away, quietly, as a moment they learned to trust you a little bit less.

And if you think you can fake it, just sprinkle in a few "mmm" noises, nod enthusiastically, and throw in the occasional "wow, that's wild"—let me stop you right there. Because fake listening *looks* fake. The eyes don't lie. The tension in your jaw, the way you cross your arms, the sigh you didn't know you let out—all of it gets picked up by the other person's nervous system before their conscious brain ever kicks in. We are wired to detect inauthenticity, even if we can't explain why someone makes us feel like our words are bouncing off a wall instead of being received by an actual person.

So, what do you do instead?

You slow the hell down.

You soften your face. You let your expressions match the emotional landscape of the conversation instead of defaulting to polite neutrality. You give just enough nods to encourage—not so many that you look like a dashboard bobblehead. You let your hands be still, or if you talk with them, you make sure they're adding to the story, not flailing like a malfunctioning windmill. You mirror, gently—not like a robot mimicking behavior, but like someone genuinely vibing with the emotional tone of the moment.

And here's the real trick—not just to listening, but to *being listened to* in return: you make your nonverbal signals consistent with your intention. If you're trying to be a safe space, *look* like one. If you're holding back judgment, don't purse your lips or furrow your brow like you're being forced to smell a lie. If you're truly present, your whole body should look like it's in the room—not like it's halfway out the door fantasizing about tacos.

This matters even more in digital settings. On Zoom? Your "I'm listening" face is now framed in a 2-inch box with lighting from hell and lag that cuts out the last three syllables of every sentence. That means you have to work harder. Turn off self-view so you stop watching your own reactions like you're a YouTuber editing a vlog. Look into the camera, not at the corner of their head. React with your face the way you would in person. And when in doubt? Say it. Out loud. "I'm listening, keep going," or "That landed—I'm just thinking." Because without body cues, words are all you've got.

The nonverbal hell yes is not about theatrics. It's about **congruence**. It's about making sure that what your face and body are saying **matches** what your words are trying to convey. It's about making it easy for people to *believe you're with them*, because they can *feel* it—not just hear it.

When your presence says yes—even without a single word—people feel safe. They keep talking. They go deeper. And that's where the magic happens.

.

Ask Questions That Don't Suck

Studies show most people forget half of what they hear within 48 hours, which wouldn't be so tragic if the average question people ask wasn't already a confusing mix of judgment, autopilot, and "I'm only asking so I can talk next."

People just don't ask questions. Not because they're stupid. Not because they don't care. But because nobody ever taught them the difference between *asking a question* and *interrogating*, between *being curious* and *being nosy*, between *creating space* and *cornering someone in it.*

We think asking a question is automatically a sign of interest or empathy, like the conversational equivalent of a warm hug. But a bad question? A lazy question? A question that's really just judgment in disguise? That lands like a slap in the face. You've been on the receiving end of that. You've felt it. Someone asks you, *"Why would you stay with someone like that?"* and boom—you're not unpacking your story anymore, you're defending your intelligence. Someone hits you with, "Are you *sure* that's what happened?" and suddenly your truth doesn't feel safe to share.

So, no, **not all questions are helpful**. Some questions shut people down harder than silence ever could.

The art of asking good questions starts with **getting out of your own ego** and actually listening to what the other person is saying—not to correct them, not to steer them, not to diagnose them, but to **understand** them, even if you don't agree, even if it makes you uncomfortable, even if it doesn't match your assumptions or agenda. And from that place—actual interest, actual connection—you can ask something that invites clarity, not compliance.

Let's break this down, because too many people confuse "being direct" with being emotionally tone-deaf. Here's how to stop doing that.

First, stop asking why when you don't want a real answer.

"Why?" seems like a harmless little word. It's even taught in every damn coaching seminar and active listening training: "Ask open-ended questions! Start with why!"

But here's the problem: "why" questions *almost always* come with a built-in undercurrent of judgment. Even when you don't mean it. Especially when you don't mean it.

"Why didn't you tell me earlier?" "Why would you put up with that?"

"Why didn't you just leave?"

Every single one of those sounds less like curiosity and more like **accusation** wrapped in a TED Talk. They put the other person on defense. They imply there's a right answer and you didn't pick it. And worst of all? They shift the conversation from connection to *explanation.* From shared space to justification.

Instead of "why," try "**what**" or "**how**." Always. They dig deeper without digging into wounds.

"What made you keep it to yourself?" "How did you handle that, honestly?"

"What was going through your head when it happened?"

Those are real questions. Human questions. Questions that say: I'm not here to judge your choices, I'm here to understand what it was like to *be* you in that moment.

Second, stop asking questions just to shift the spotlight.

You ever ask someone how they're doing and then immediately follow it up with your own story before they even finish their first sentence?

"How's work?" "Yeah, same here, it's been insane—I had like ten meetings back-to-back and then—"

You didn't ask a question. You set a trap. You used curiosity as a placeholder until you could steer it back to yourself. And listen, we've *all* done it. Especially when we're tired, emotionally overloaded, or just socially checked out. But that habit—asking for someone's truth and then bulldozing it with your own? That's not connection. That's conversational kleptomania. Stop stealing the mic.

Ask a question. Then *shut up* and let the silence do some work. If they pause? Let it be awkward. If they hesitate? That's not your cue to rescue them from discomfort—it's a sign that something real might be trying to surface. Give it room.

Third, get better at reading the room before asking deeper questions.

Context matters. Energy matters. If someone just told you something painful or messy or loaded and you immediately go full therapist mode with, "So, what do you think that says about your attachment style?"—you're not being insightful. You're being intrusive.

Some moments call for curiosity. Some moments call for stillness. Some moments call for letting the other person decide how deep they want to go.

Ask questions like you're knocking on a door, not kicking it open.

Instead of:

"Do you think that's because your dad never emotionally validated you?"

Try:

"Can I ask something that might be a little personal?" "Do you want to talk more about that or do you just need me to listen?"

"Is this one of those times you need empathy or distraction?"

Now *that's* emotional intelligence. That's grace. That's knowing how to ask without demanding.

Fourth, know that some of the best questions are short and simple and weirdly gentle.

You don't need to be eloquent. You don't need to sound like a podcast host. You just need to *care enough to pause before you speak.*

Here are a few that never miss:

- "What do you need right now?"
- "Do you want to talk about it or just sit in it for a bit?"
- "Want me to just listen or are you looking for ideas?"
- "Can I ask what you're feeling underneath that?"
- "Is this something you want to unpack or just name out loud and move on?"

These don't sound profound. But they work because they respect agency. They hand the steering wheel back to the person who's feeling the thing. They don't demand vulnerability—they *invite* it.

The truth is, asking better questions isn't about mastering a script or memorizing some coaching template. It's about listening hard enough to ask something real. It's about checking your ego at the door, resisting the urge to prove how emotionally intelligent you are, and instead showing that you're curious—not controlling. Present—not performative.

And if that sounds like work? It is. But it's the kind that pays off in every relationship you care about.

Because once people figure out that talking to you doesn't come with a risk of being judged, redirected, interrogated, or hijacked—they'll start telling you the truth. Not the polished version. The real one.

And that's where connection actually begins.

The Mirror Effect

You ever talk to someone and feel like they actually *get* you—like you didn't have to overexplain, or backtrack, or justify every feeling you just laid bare? That's not magic. That's **mirroring**. And no, it's not the creepy kind where someone mimics your every move like a glitchy AI trying to blend in. It's the emotional kind. The kind where you speak and they reflect something back that makes you feel **less alone** inside your own damn experience. And when it's done right, it's not flashy, and it's not deep-voiced or dramatic—it's quiet, warm, sometimes awkward, but always real.

The mirror effect is what makes people **feel heard**—not just listened to. It's what turns a conversation from a tennis match of ideas into a real connection. Because here's what most people miss: **listening isn't about proving you understand. It's about helping *them* understand that *you're trying.***

And the best way to do that isn't by interrupting with your own story or paraphrasing them like a motivational speaker. It's by holding up a gentle mirror that shows: I see you. I hear what you're saying. I'm not twisting it. I'm not fixing it. I'm just handing it back so *you* can see it, too.

That can be as simple as saying:

- ***"It sounds like that really caught you off guard."***
- ***"You didn't feel supported in that moment."***
- ***"You were holding it together, but underneath, you were unraveling."***

These aren't lines you script out. They come from actually being *with* the person—tracking their tone, their pacing, their emotion, and offering back a version of what they said that captures the heart of it, not just the words.

What you're doing in that moment is **reflection**, not rerouting. You're not making it about you. You're not hijacking the spotlight to tell them how *you* once went through something similar, or how *you* coped, or how *you* think they should feel. You're simply placing their emotion back in their hands—gently, respectfully, like it's fragile and important—so they feel less like a lunatic for having it in the first place.

That's emotional generosity. That's relational maturity. That's communication with a backbone and a heartbeat.

I just want to make sure you understand that **mirroring isn't about parroting.** Nobody wants to feel like they're in therapy when they're just trying to have a normal human moment. If you repeat everything they say like a hostage negotiator, you'll sound like a robot doing improv.

It's not:

"So, what I'm hearing is you're frustrated, sad, and feeling disconnected."

No one wants to be handled. They want to be heard. And there's a massive difference between parroting back emotional keywords and *actually capturing* what's being felt beneath them. Mirroring isn't about showing off your emotional vocabulary—it's about making the other person feel **more seen** than they did before they opened their mouth.

And sometimes? Sometimes mirroring is just sitting there with your eyebrows raised and your lips pressed together like, "Damn, that's heavy."

No words. Just alignment. Just *being with* someone instead of managing their experience.

That's the core of it. Mirroring is about *presence,* not performance.

It's why saying "I get it" can fall flat when you clearly don't. It's why "Wow, that must've been hard" hits differently when your tone and face actually *match* the weight of what's being shared. And it's why someone would rather hear ***"I don't have words, but I'm here,"*** than some well-intentioned mini-speech about how they're strong and it'll all be okay.

People don't want speeches. They want signals. Signals that tell them you're still with them, you haven't mentally left the room, you're not trying to push them out of their own story just because it's making you squirm.

And yes, this matters in digital conversations too. Especially in text, where there's no tone, no timing, no face to react to. That's where you have to be *really* intentional. Don't just reply with a thumbs-up or a vague "yikes." Reflect their language back to them. Use their words, but soften the edges. Echo the emotional vibe, not just the content.

"That sounds like it completely threw you off."

"I don't blame you for feeling that way."

"Yeah, that's a lot, and you're allowed to feel all of it."

You're not cosigning drama. You're acknowledging reality.

That's what mirroring does. It lets the other person exhale. It helps them feel less like they're broadcasting into a void. And it **builds trust**, fast, because they don't feel judged or managed or pitied—they feel **understood**.

And once someone feels understood, they start telling you the *real* stuff.

Because **nobody opens up fully until they know they're not going to be dropped halfway through the landing.** Mirroring tells them it's safe to land.

So, if you want to become the kind of person people confide in—the kind of communicator who doesn't just hear, but *lands* with people—start using that mirror. Gently. Sparingly. Authentically.

Don't steal the moment. Reflect it.

That's how you build connection.

That's how you earn trust.

And that's how you shut up and *actually* listen.

CHAPTER 3:

Listening Under Fire

(How Not to Flinch, Fume, or Freak Out When Conversations Get Hard)

The words might stay polite, but your body's already declared a war

Stay in the Room When Your Ego Tries to Bolt

There's a moment that happens in almost every emotionally loaded conversation—a split second, maybe even shorter, when something hits you the wrong way, when your stomach tightens, when your heart picks up speed, when your brain goes from curious to cornered, and in that moment, your ego starts reaching for the emergency exit. You feel it in your chest. You feel it in your jaw. You feel it in the way your entire nervous system suddenly flips from "I'm listening" to "I need to get the hell out of this without looking like a jerk."

Maybe it was a criticism. Maybe it was a tone. Maybe it was someone saying, "Can I give you some feedback?" in the same voice someone might use to say, "There's something in your teeth." Whatever it is, something inside you flares, and your first impulse isn't to stay grounded. It's to *defend.* Or deflect. Or shut down. Or retreat into overexplaining. Or fling the conversational grenade back in their direction so you don't have to sit in the discomfort for one more goddamn second.

And that, my friend? **That's exactly the moment you have to catch yourself.**

Because that's not truth talking. That's your *ego*, and ego doesn't want to understand. Ego wants to *win.*

But here's something you won't hear in most communication books: if you can't stay in the room when your pride's been poked or your image takes a hit or your flaws are suddenly on the table where everyone can see them—you're not ready for real connection. You're not ready for intimacy. You're not ready for leadership. Because none of those things exist without the capacity to **sit in discomfort** without making it someone else's fault.

So, let's talk about what actually happens in those moments, because if you want to get better at high-stakes communication, you have to get honest about what your brain and body are doing *before* your mouth catches up.

When someone says something that triggers you—especially if it feels like a judgment, a rejection, or a threat to how you see yourself—your nervous system lights up like a cheap neon sign in a bad part of town. **Fight, flight, freeze,** or **fix**. That's the menu. And before you can even decide what you want, your body's already ordered it for you.

Maybe you get hot and snappy—*fight mode.* You interrupt, raise your voice, throw sarcasm like daggers, not because you're a monster but because that edge makes you feel momentarily back in control.

Or maybe you mentally check out—*flight mode.* You smile, nod, pretend to listen, but inside you've already started drafting the email you'll write later to correct everything that just happened.

Some of us go *freeze.* We blank. We shut down. We hear the words but can't process them. We get that weird tunnel vision like we're watching ourselves from across the room and thinking, "I have absolutely no idea how to respond without making this worse."

And then there's *fix mode*—my personal favorite. Where you immediately jump into problem-solving so you don't have to sit in the discomfort of just feeling what you're feeling. You say things like, "Okay, well, I'll do better," or "Got it, I'll fix it," not because you've processed the feedback but because you want the awkwardness to end as fast as humanly possible.

All of that? It's normal. It's human. It's your nervous system doing what it was built to do. But if you want to be a powerful communicator—*especially* when shit gets real—you have to learn how to notice those responses *without letting them run the show.*

That starts with recognizing your "exit cues."

Everyone has them. The moment your breathing changes. The way your voice gets clipped. The way your arms cross. The way you suddenly "have to pee" in the middle of a tense conversation. Whatever your move is, you've done it before. You've bailed on the moment. And you've probably told yourself afterward that it was just too much, or that the other person was being unreasonable, or that they wouldn't have listened anyway. And maybe sometimes that's true. But maybe other times… you just **didn't know how to stay**.

Staying isn't passive. It's not just sitting still while you get emotionally whacked in the face. It's *active restraint.* It's saying to yourself, "I'm triggered, but I'm not going to react yet." It's letting that spike of cortisol run its course without grabbing the mic and going off. It's listening *even though every part of you wants to argue, clarify, correct, or disappear.*

And that takes practice. It takes the ability to pause—not to punish yourself, not to become some silent martyr, but to *interrupt the autopilot reaction* that would normally sabotage the whole conversation. That pause? That's where the power is.

Because here's what you learn, once you train yourself to pause and stay instead of running or retaliating: **most of the time, the thing that triggered you wasn't actually an attack.** It was someone else being messy, being clumsy, or simply being human. Maybe they didn't deliver their point with perfect compassion. Maybe their tone sucked. Maybe they had no idea how vulnerable they just made you feel. But that doesn't mean you have to go to war. That doesn't mean you need to shut down. That doesn't mean you need to immediately rebuild your sense of self by making *them* the villain.

Staying in the room means holding your ground *without making it a battlefield.*

It means saying, "Okay, that hit harder than I expected," instead of "Wow, that's really unfair."

It means saying, "Can I have a second to think about this?" instead of scrambling to fix something you haven't even fully heard yet.

It means giving yourself enough time to figure out whether you're hurt because you were mistreated—or just because your pride got bruised.

It doesn't make you weak. It makes you dangerous in all the right ways. Because once you learn to sit with discomfort without reacting, without collapsing, without throwing a doody back at them—you become the kind of person other people can bring hard truths to. And that's rare. That's powerful. That's leadership.

So, the next time you feel the urge to shut down or bite back or escape the moment, don't shame yourself. Just name it. Notice it. And then do the most radical thing possible in that moment: **stay**.

Feedback Isn't a Threat (Unless You Make It One)

Feedback. That glorious word that's supposed to help us grow, learn, evolve, and yet somehow still feels like stepping into traffic every time someone says, *"Hey, can I give you some feedback?"* Because what they mean is: *I have thoughts about how you're doing life, and I'm about to tell you even if you didn't ask.* It's like emotional surprise surgery—no anesthetic, no prep, just vibes.

But know this: **feedback isn't inherently bad**. It's not a threat. It's not an attack. It's not a declaration that you're broken. It's information. It's someone handing you their perception of you—clumsily, awkwardly, sometimes a little too loudly, but still, just a perception.

And if you can learn to take it *without treating it like a personal betrayal*, you'll have an unfair advantage in every room you walk into. Because most people? They fall apart the second someone doesn't clap for them. One mildly critical sentence and suddenly they're spiraling through every insecurity they've ever buried under productivity and self-deprecating jokes.

But you? You are the lucky one, you have this book. So, let's fix it. Let's get brutally honest about why feedback hits so hard and how to stop reacting like someone just slapped your inner child with a performance review.

First off: feedback is not a personality test

It's not about your worth. It's not about your value as a person. It's not a diagnosis of your deepest flaws.

"You interrupted a lot in that meeting" ≠ "You're a selfish, obnoxious nightmare who deserves to live in a cave."

It just means… you interrupted. You got excited. Or nervous. Or didn't read the room. That's it. It's a behavior. And guess what? **Behaviors can be changed**. Not because you suck. But because sometimes your default settings need an update.

You are not your worst habit. You're just someone who occasionally misses the mark like every other carbon-based life form. Calm down now, would ya?

Second: your ego hears everything louder than it actually is

You know how when someone says: "We need to talk," your brain immediately flashes back to every questionable decision you've made since 2009?

Yeah. That.

Your ego is wired to protect your self-image like a guard dog hopped up on Red Bull. The second it senses criticism—even gentle, constructive, "I'm only telling you this because I care" kind of criticism—it goes feral. And suddenly, you're not in a conversation. You're in a courtroom. And you're the defendant *and* the lawyer *and* the bailiff, all at once.

So, what do you do instead?

You train yourself to **hear the message, not the delivery**. Because yeah, maybe their tone was a little sharp. Maybe their timing was garbage. Maybe they sandwiched it between two compliments and still managed to make you feel like a failure.

Still. Try to listen *past* that.

What are they actually trying to say?

- That you talk too fast and they feel steamrolled?
- That your emails come off passive-aggressive?
- That you dominate meetings without realizing it?

Fine. Sit with that. You don't have to agree with every word. You just have to be *open enough* to consider the parts that might be true. **Might**. Not *definitely*. But if three people have said it and you're still convinced it's them and not you… maybe check again.

Third: you're allowed to pause before responding

Just because someone delivers feedback doesn't mean you owe them a perfectly gracious response in 0.4 seconds. This isn't a TED Talk. You're not a feedback-response vending machine.

You're allowed to say:

- "I'm taking that in. Give me a sec."
- "That's hard to hear, but I appreciate you saying it."

- "I need to process this before I respond properly."

That's not weak. That's **maturity**. That's what grown-ups do when their nervous system is screaming but their higher self is like, *"Please don't say something petty right now, we're trying to evolve here."*

Buy yourself time. Let the sting settle. Ask clarifying questions if you're unclear.

"Can you give me an example of when I did that?"

"What impact did it have on you?"

"What would have landed better?"

Boom. Now you sound like a professional, emotionally intelligent wizard—even if you're low-key dissociating inside.

Fourth: don't weaponize self-awareness to avoid responsibility

There's a temptation, especially for smart, reflective people, to respond to feedback with a kind of *intellectualized deflection* that sounds like accountability but is actually just a dodge.

You know what I mean.

- "Yeah, I know I do that. I'm working on it."
- "It's my anxiety, I can't help it."
- "I've been told that before."

Okay. But are you *doing* anything about it? Or are you just using self-awareness as a shield, so you don't have to feel the sting of growth?

Knowing your patterns is not the same as changing them.

Take the feedback. Say thank you. Decide if it's useful. And if it is? Do something about it.

Final thought: not all feedback is holy

I'm sure you know that without me telling you, but… drumroll… some people are just bad at giving feedback. Jaw drop, I know. But they project. They unload. They critique things that are none of their business. Not all feedback is useful or fair. **But the fact that it stung? That's data.**

You can thank someone for their feedback *without adopting their entire worldview*. You can say, "That's not how I see it, but I'll think about it." That's not defensive. That's called being a person with boundaries and a brain.

The point of feedback isn't to make you feel small. It's to give you *insight*—into how you come across, how people experience you, where your blind spots are. And if you can take it without melting down, you're ahead of 90% of people walking around pretending they want growth but combusting the second they're asked to look in a mirror.

So, next time it comes your way?

Don't flinch. Don't fight. Don't flee.

Just stay curious. Stay calm. Stay open long enough to learn something—even if what you learn is just, "Wow, I'm actually handling this better than I used to."

That counts too.

What to Do When Someone's Coming in Hot

You're sitting there, maybe trying to work, maybe just existing peacefully, and suddenly—boom. Someone's energy slams into you like a truck. They're ranting. Venting. Crying. Snapping. Blaming. Or maybe they're not even raising their voice, but the tension is thick enough to taste and they're clearly not okay. And now their emotional hurricane has made *you* ground zero.

It doesn't matter if it's a partner, a coworker, your mom, or your best friend mid-spiral. When someone's coming in hot, it's easy to freeze, freak out, or say something dumb just to get the discomfort to end. You go into survival mode. You try to fix it. Or you defend yourself. Or you emotionally shut down and nod like a hostage in your own living room. Anything to make the storm stop.

But here's the thing: reacting out of panic doesn't de-escalate anything. In fact, it almost always makes it worse. And if you're going to be someone who communicates like a grown-ass adult, you have to learn how to **hold your ground** when someone else's emotions are trying to knock you over.

I just want you to be clear: when someone's upset and they come to you loud, messy, intense, or raw—it's not always an attack. Sometimes, it's just leakage. Their emotional bandwidth has been stretched to the limit, and you're the first safe place they've had to let it out. Sometimes that's a compliment. Sometimes it's a red flag. But in either case, you're now in a moment where how *you* respond is going to decide what happens next.

And no, "shutting it down" or "walking away" isn't always the answer. Yes, boundaries exist. Yes, you're allowed to not engage with abusive, toxic, or manipulative outbursts. But most of the time, we're not talking about verbal warfare. We're talking about people we love or work with or care about who are just overwhelmed, dysregulated, or struggling, and who are asking, sometimes in a completely sideways, emotionally chaotic way, for connection.

So, here's how you deal with it without turning into a sponge, a doormat, or a brick wall.

First of all, don't match the volume

This is the trap. They're intense, so you rise to meet them. They're agitated, so you stiffen. They throw heat, so you throw it right back because you feel cornered. That's how arguments explode. That's how people say things they regret. That's how emotional grenades turn living rooms into emotional battlefields.

Instead, **lower your volume**. **Slow your voice down**. Make it clear with your *tone* that you're not entering the chaos. You're not dismissing it. You're just not *matching it.* You are not obligated to rise to their temperature. You're allowed to stay where you are.

That calm, grounded energy? That's leadership. And it's contagious. **People will mirror it—eventually—if you hold it.**

Second, validate the emotion, not the delivery

Someone doesn't need to say it perfectly to be feeling something real. And if you're sitting there waiting for them to word it nicely before you'll engage, congratulations—you're now arguing about grammar while the actual problem is bleeding out on the floor.

You can acknowledge the emotion without cosigning the story.

You can say:

- "You're clearly upset, and I want to hear why."
- "I'm not okay with how this is being said, but I can see that you're hurting."
- "Let's slow this down. I care. I'm listening. Let's not go to war."

You don't need to fix them. You don't need to defend yourself. You need to show that you're **present**. That's it. That alone will shift the energy.

Third, don't absorb what's not yours

When someone vents, especially if it's someone you care about, the instinct is to help carry the load. But there's a difference between **holding space** and **inhaling their emotional chaos like secondhand smoke**.

Their pain isn't your fault just because you're nearby and their overwhelm isn't your responsibility to solve. You can care deeply without making yourself the emotional garbage bin for every unprocessed feeling they're tossing out.

So, how do you stay present without absorbing it?

You ground yourself. You breathe slower. You plant your feet. You listen with boundaries. You remind yourself—internally, silently—that **they are allowed to feel this,** and **you are allowed to stay steady**. You don't need to shut them down. You just need to stay centered long enough for them to come back to earth.

Fourth, don't defend yourself until you've actually heard them

This is the hardest part. When someone's angry *at you*, your brain throws up a thousand little protest signs. "That's not what I meant!" "That's not fair!" "You're twisting it!" All of them might be valid. But if you fire them off before you've even let the other person finish, you don't look confident—you look reactive. You look guilty. You look like someone who can't take a hit without flailing.

You want power? Try this instead:

- "Okay. Keep going."
- "That stung a little, but I want to understand where you're coming from."
- "I didn't expect to hear that, but I'm still here."

You don't have to agree. You just have to **stay**.

And then, once they've landed, once the dust has settled, once they're no longer foaming at the mouth or crying into their hoodie—you can speak your piece. Calmly. Clearly. In full control of your side of the street. That's when it actually lands.

Last: it's not your job to regulate them, but it is your responsibility to regulate *yourself*

You are not the emotional babysitter. You don't have to fix their tone or stop them from unraveling. But you do have to decide what kind of communicator **you want to be** in the heat of the moment.

If you want to be someone who listens with grace, with grit, with grounded presence—you can't do that from inside your own emotional panic room. You've got to stay in your body, stay in the moment, and remember: they're not the enemy. Their tone isn't the truth. And how you respond matters *more* than how they came in.

Because the truth is, most people aren't actually asking you to solve anything when they come in hot. They're asking, *Can you handle me right now? Can you hear me without flinching? Can you stay without shutting down?*

And if you can?

You become the safest person in the room.

Disarm With Curiosity

Here's the secret to staying calm when someone's losing it: **don't try to control them. Try to *understand* them.**

Because the moment you stop trying to dominate, fix, explain, or outmaneuver someone in a heated conversation, and start getting **curious** instead—everything changes. You move from being an emotional target to being a stable point of contact. A mirror. A map. A weird, unexpected island of calm in the middle of someone else's hurricane.

And no, this doesn't mean you become soft or submissive. Curiosity is not compliance. It's not "just take the abuse and smile." It's not "be the bigger person" in the way that usually just means "be quiet and don't make waves." It's about shifting your power from **reaction** to **observation**. From "this hurts, I need to hit back" to "this is intense, and I want to know what's under it."

You're not escaping the moment. You're **entering it differently.**

Because when someone's being aggressive, irrational, sarcastic, or defensive, it's easy to take the bait. They say something cutting and you instantly want to defend yourself, correct them, drag out a PowerPoint of receipts. But when you meet force with force, the conversation collapses into a contest. And once you're in that ring, no one's listening. Everyone's just swinging.

So, don't swing.

Get curious.

Ask questions that slow things down

The best way to derail emotional chaos without going to war is to ask a question. Not a rhetorical slap, not a gotcha line, not "Oh really? And where exactly do *you* think you're being reasonable?" But a real question. One that shifts the tone. One that creates space.

Try these:

- "What's the part that's hitting you the hardest right now?"
- "Can you tell me what this feels like from your side?"
- "Do you want to walk me through what led up to this?"
- "What are you actually needing from me right now—underneath the frustration?"

These aren't fancy. They're just unexpected. Because most people in conflict are used to being argued with, not **invited** to explain.

And the moment you ask a question that **doesn't** escalate the situation? You're rewiring the rhythm of the whole conversation.

Curiosity is not approval—it's control

Let's be clear: asking questions in a heated moment doesn't mean you're validating bad behavior or letting someone off the hook. It just means you're **choosing not to react like they expected you to**.

That alone makes you unpredictable. And unpredictability, when used calmly and kindly, is one of the fastest ways to interrupt someone else's defensiveness.

Think about it—when someone comes in ready to argue and you don't argue back, you've taken away their fuel. They were ready for a fight. They had their opening statement loaded. And now you're asking, "What's the story behind that?" and their brain short-circuits, experiencing the 'can't compute' moment. They were gearing up for a power struggle, not a dialogue.

And guess what? Most people would rather be *understood* than *win*. Even if they don't admit it. Even if they act like they want to crush you with their logic and come out on top. **Deep down, most people just want to be heard.** Curiosity gets you there faster than any well-crafted counterpoint ever could.

Match before you lead

Back in Chapter 2, we talked about **The Mirror Effect**—that powerful move where you reflect back what someone's saying to help them feel seen. That was about building connection. This is about **steering a high-intensity moment without escalating it**.

In emotionally loaded conversations, mirroring becomes less about reflecting feelings and more about **calibrating the emotional temperature** in the room. It's subtle, and it's strategic. You're not copying their energy—you're **meeting it just enough** to build trust, and then guiding it somewhere more constructive.

It works like this:

- If they're talking fast and loud, you don't whisper back. You stay calm, but you don't flatten out completely—you match enough of their intensity to show presence.
- If their body's tight and upright, you ground your own without going limp—so you're steady, not passive.
- If they're using charged language, you acknowledge the charge without absorbing it:
- "Yeah, I hear how fired up you are about this, and it makes sense."

You mirror to **stabilize**, then **slowly lead**.

It's emotional aikido. They throw energy at you. You don't block it, and you don't return fire. You absorb, pivot, and redirect.

This is next-level listening—not just for connection, but for control. Quiet control. The kind that doesn't need to overpower the moment, because it knows how to **hold it steady until the storm passes.**

Be curious even when you're right

This is the real ego killer. You know you're right. You **know for sure** the facts are on your side. You're being calm, rational, thoughtful, and they're spiraling like a raccoon in a vending machine. But if you shove your correctness in their face like a trophy, you've lost the point.

Curiosity keeps you open even when you've technically "won." Because being right doesn't mean you've been **heard**. And if you don't create space for the other person to land emotionally, your point might be flawless and still feel like a personal attack.

So, ask:

- "What part still feels unresolved to you?"
- "Is there something I've missed that would help this land better for you?"
- "I'm clear on my side, but I want to make sure I'm not blind to yours."

That's not weakness. That's *mastery*.

Final reminder: curiosity is your way out of the storm

When the conversation feels like it's sliding into the gutter, when you're tempted to yell, correct, storm out, or shut down—ask a question instead.

It doesn't have to be deep. It just has to be real.

Because the moment you shift into curiosity, you're no longer reacting. You're leading. Quietly and calmly. Without forcing it.

And that's the kind of communication power no one sees coming, but everyone remembers.

Listening Is Stronger Than Winning

There's a specific flavor of self-satisfaction that comes from verbally body-slamming someone mid-argument with that one line you *know* they won't come back from—you've built it, rehearsed it, honed it in the back of your mind while pretending to listen, and then when the moment comes, you drop it like it's hot, mic metaphorically in hand, already fantasizing about the applause you absolutely won't get because now the other person is either sulking, crying, or way too stunned to say anything, and you're standing there like, **Why does this still feel like shit?**

Because it does. It always does.

Even when you're right, even when they were out of line or started it. Even when you "won."

Winning is such a seductive little gremlin in conversations. It sits in the corner of your brain clapping its grubby little hands every time you score a point, every time you out-logic someone or push them into that "fine, whatever" corner where they stop fighting not because they understand, but because they're emotionally tired and they want out. You feel momentarily powerful. Maybe even smug. And then about thirty seconds later you feel like a bit of an ass. Or worse—**they do**. And you're left wondering why you always seem to get the last word but never the outcome you actually wanted.

Because here's the thing no one teaches us when we're learning to "communicate effectively": **you don't get points for being louder, faster, or more articulate. You get impact.** Or you don't. And impact has nothing to do with scoring intellectual touchdowns and everything to do with whether the other person walked away from the conversation feeling heard, respected, maybe even a little bit changed. That part? That happens when you *listen*. Not when you dazzle.

But nobody tells you that. Instead, you're taught to gear up. Debate team tactics. Cross-examination energy. Who's got receipts. Who's more "emotionally evolved." Who remembered to say "I feel" instead of "You always." And yet somehow, despite all that skill and vocabulary and awareness and insight—you still find yourself in arguments that end in silence, eye rolls, or emotional hangovers that last all weekend.

And you know why?

Because you were trying to win. And **they** were trying to survive you.

There's a difference.

There's a massive, life-altering, relationship-saving difference between **being right** and **being reachable**. Between making your point and actually being **heard**. Between "they admitted I was right" and "they felt safe enough to open up."

And I get it. You've worked hard to be able to express yourself clearly. You've probably had to claw your way out of years of not being taken seriously, or not being allowed to have an opinion, or constantly being told you're too sensitive or too aggressive or too much of whatever the hell people said when they didn't want to deal with your actual perspective. So, yeah—now that you've found your voice, you want to use it. You want to *defend* it. You want to make damn sure that if someone comes at you sideways, you'll be able to meet them, line for line, beat for beat, and not back down.

I get it. I do.

But I'm also telling you this: the next level of power—the level most people never reach—is not in how well you speak. It's in **how well you listen when you're under fire** and your ego is screaming but you *don't* interrupt. You *don't* correct. You *don't* over-explain. You don't pull out the receipts even though they're right there in your notes app and they're color-coded and you've been waiting for this day for months.

You breathe. You lean back. And you say, "Okay. Keep going."

That moment right there? That's **strength**. Not the loud kind. Not the fancy Instagram-quote kind. The quiet, almost boring kind. The kind that doesn't need to win because it already knows its worth.

Listening when it's easy isn't a skill. It's a mood. Listening when it's hard—when everything in you wants to fight, fix, flee, or fire off a three-paragraph text with bullet points and emotional callouts? That's the work. **That's where your self-respect gets built**. Not just because you stayed calm, but because you **chose** not to burn the house down just to prove you had a match.

And no, I'm not saying you let people walk all over you. I'm not saying you don't set boundaries or push back or say your piece. I'm saying you **stop pretending that "winning" the moment is worth losing the connectio**n. Because nine times out of ten? It's not. It never was. And the people who can't hear you aren't going to suddenly get it because you phrased your argument with more precision and panache.

They're going to get it when they realize you're not trying to win—you're trying to *understand*. You're not coming at them—you're standing *with* them. And sometimes, the only way they're going to figure that out is if you stop pushing and just let the silence hold for a second. Let the message land without a tagline. Let the energy settle without commentary.

That's how trust starts.

That's how influence begins.

That's how you become the kind of person people actually *listen* to—even when they don't want to. Even when it hurts. Even when they came in swinging and left wondering why they suddenly feel safer than they did before.

Because you didn't try to win. You just stayed. And you *listened.*

And that is stronger than anything you could've said.

So, if you've made it this far and you're still with me—still breathing, still not rage-spiraling, still not plotting your next verbal takedown in a group chat—congrats. You've just learned how to stay in hard conversations without burning down the building.

Now let's talk about what happens when it's **your** turn to speak.

Because listening will make people trust you.

But what you say when the silence ends is what makes them **follow** you.

CHAPTER 4:
Confidence You Can Hear

Everyone's winging it—some people are just better at pretending they're not.

What Confidence Actually Sounds Like (It's Not Volume)

If you've read **Stop Overthinking**, you already know that real confidence doesn't look like chest-puffing, loud-talking, corner-dominating energy.

(Haven't read it yet? Scan this QR code to grab your copy →)

It doesn't scream. It doesn't perform. And it damn sure doesn't come from repeating "I am powerful" in the mirror while your coffee's burning and your hair looks like a rejected audition for a Pantene commercial. Confidence isn't that dramatic. **It's quieter. Heavier. It lands.**

And when it comes to communication—especially the kind that makes people shut up and *listen*—confidence doesn't sound like a motivational speaker on fast-forward. It sounds calm. It sounds clear. It sounds like someone who *isn't trying to convince you of anything*, because they already believe themselves.

You know what doesn't sound confident? Talking so fast you start swallowing your own words like they're late for a train. Or apologizing for your opinion before you've even shared it. Or adding three question marks to every sentence because you're hoping to come off "friendly" and not "intimidating." (**cough*… they're not intimidated. They're confused.)

Confidence has weight. You can hear it in someone's tone before they've even said something important. And no, it's not just about having a deep voice or a perfect accent or that irritating ability to never say "um." It's about how someone *owns their air*. How they take a second to think before they speak—not because they're scared, but because they **don't need to fill the space to prove they belong in it.**

Let me give you a real-life example.

I once sat through a Zoom meeting (well, MS Teams in my case, but who cares) where two people were pitching the same idea. One came in hot—fast-talking, loud, borderline breathless like she was in a one-person episode of Shark Tank. She had slides. She had stats. She had the energy of someone who was both trying to impress and terrified they wouldn't. The second person? No slides. Just leaned in, made eye contact with the camera, and said: "Here's what I think will actually work, and here's why." Short pause. No rush. No filler. **And everyone leaned in.** You could feel the room shift. And it wasn't because the second pitch was *better*. It was because the delivery said, "I trust what I'm about to say, and you probably should too."

Confidence lives in that pause. That breath. That moment where you could keep talking, but you don't. Because you know the silence isn't a threat—it's part of your message.

And let's talk about **tone**, because this is where people get real weird. Some folks think confidence sounds like volume. Like if they say it louder, it'll land harder. But yelling is usually a sign someone's already lost the plot and is trying to claw their way back to relevance. True confidence often *drops the volume.* It settles. It doesn't have to dominate the space—it *anchors* it.

There's this trick I use when I feel like I'm spiraling in a conversation—when I feel rushed or nervous or like I'm shrinking mid-sentence. I literally stop and **lower my voice by just one notch**. Not dramatically. Just enough to hear myself again. It's like an instant power reset. Suddenly I remember, *oh right—I'm not here to prove anything. I'm here because I have something to say.* Try it. It works.

Now, I'm not going to pretend that all of this is easy, especially when you're new in a room, or outclassed on paper, or sitting across from someone with more money, more experience, or more people nodding when they talk. That's when the imposter voice starts up: *You shouldn't be here. Don't screw it up. Say it fast so no one interrupts you.*

But here's the thing. Rushing doesn't protect you from judgment. It *guarantees* it. **People listen to those who sound like they believe what they're saying.** And belief doesn't sound like panic. It doesn't sound like backpedaling. It doesn't sound like "just real quick..." or "this might be dumb, but..." or "I don't know if this is right..."—because by the time you've coughed up your point through all those disclaimers, nobody's taking it seriously. Least of all you.

I'm not saying you have to speak in slow-motion TED Talk cadence. I'm saying: give your words enough room to breathe. Stop rushing to get it out. Stop apologizing mid-thought. Stop talking over yourself in an effort to soften the blow.

If your confidence is still fragile, that's fine. That's real. But don't let your *voice* carry your doubt for you. It's not responsible for babysitting your self-esteem.

If you need a crutch, use breath. Use pace. Use silence. **Say your piece, and then *shut up and let it sit.*** Let them process it. Let them respond. And if they interrupt, or talk over you, or try to hijack the moment, that's fine too. You still said what you came to say. And that's power.

Confidence doesn't come from sounding bulletproof. It comes from sounding *clear*. Even if your voice shakes. Even if you're nervous. Even if you're not sure how it's landing. It comes from trusting that what you have to say is worth saying—even if you don't tie it in a bow.

And when that kind of voice walks into a room—low, steady, no fluff—you better believe people notice.

Verbal Tics That Undermine Your Authority

There's nothing quite like watching someone walk into a conversation with a solid point—something smart, relevant, maybe even a little brave, and then immediately watch them shoot it in the kneecap with five layers of verbal fluff, three disclaimers, and a nervous giggle that practically screams, *"Please don't hate me for existing."*

We've all done it. I've done it. You've done it. Your boss has done it. The person giving that presentation you sat through last week with the 87 "just real quick"s and "I might be totally wrong here, but…" has *definitely* done it.

These aren't mistakes because you're weak. **These are survival tactics.** Learned habits. Built-in apology systems designed to protect you from the possibility of being misunderstood, disliked, or—God forbid—perceived as *confident on purpose.*

And they need to go.

Not because you should start talking like a corporate assassin or a life coach hopped up on turmeric and LinkedIn memes. But because the way you frame your message tells people **whether to believe you before they've even heard what you said.**

Let's break down the biggest culprits.

"Does that make sense?" (a.k.a. the Backpedal Classic)

This one usually sneaks in at the *end* of an otherwise solid statement. You're mid-flow, you've laid out your idea clearly, and then you undercut it with, "Does that make sense?" like you're not sure your audience can read above a fifth-grade level or like you're asking permission to keep speaking.

Come on, unless you've been rambling like a conspiracy theorist on Red Bull with a side of Ritalin, *it does make sense.* And if it doesn't, they'll ask. You don't need to babysit their comprehension. You're not a human CliffsNotes.

Try:

- "Let me know if you want to dig into that further."
- "I'm happy to clarify anything that's unclear."
- Or better yet, just *shut up and wait.*

"Sorry, just..." / "I might be wrong, but..."

These are the voice-cracking disclaimers we use to soften the blow of our own opinions. It's like bubble-wrapping your thoughts in case someone decides to throw them back at you.

And look, I get it. You don't want to come off arrogant. You want to sound approachable. But confidence without humility isn't the problem here. **Timidity disguised as politeness is.**

Every time you start a sentence with "Sorry, just..." you're shrinking before you've even stood up. You're putting yourself in the role of someone who needs to ask permission to speak—**even when you've been invited to speak.**

Try:

- "Here's what I'm seeing."
- "What stands out to me is this…"
- "This might be unpopular, but here's where I'm landing."

Those sound firm. Clear. Still human. No apology required.

"I could be wrong, but…"

This is my personal favorite. It's like emotional insurance. You're not sure they'll agree with you, so you **pre-discredit yourself to stay likable**.

Except now you've made it real easy for them to disregard your idea entirely. You basically handed them a user manual for how to ignore you. Don't do that.

Here's what you say instead:

- "I'm open to being challenged on this, but here's how I'm thinking about it."
- "This is my current perspective—happy to shift if I'm off."
- Or the magic: "Here's where I'm landing right now."

Boom. That's flexible confidence. Not defensive. Not arrogant. Just solid ground with a soft edge.

"Real quick…" / "I'll just take a second…"

These are the phrases we use when we don't want to feel like we're taking up too much space. Which is wild, because most of the time, nobody else in the room is thinking that. *You're the one thinking it.*

You say "real quick" to preempt imagined judgment. You say "just a second" like you're borrowing someone's time and you're afraid of the late fees. But when you do that, you signal that what you're about to say isn't worth much—so why should anyone else think it is?

Try:

- "Let me add something here."
- "Here's a quick angle I want to share."
- Or skip the intro entirely and just say the thing.

Don't talk yourself out of authority before you've even opened your mouth.

How do you fix this?

First: **Start by noticing**. You don't need to launch a war on every verbal tic overnight. Just start listening to your own voice. Your patterns. When you do it. Around whom. What situations bring out your disclaimer reflex.

Second: **Pick one phrase** to eliminate. That's it. Just one. Choose your worst offender. "I'm sorry, but…"? "Does that make sense?" Kill it. Murder it with intention. Replace it with nothing if you're not sure what else to say.

Third: **Practice in low-stakes settings**. With friends. In emails. On voice memos. In that Monday morning team huddle that no one pays full attention to anyway. Train your mouth to stop sending signals that your words are optional.

And remember: you're not being rude by speaking plainly. You're not being cocky by cutting the fluff. You're not being harsh by leaving out the little fake-apology bows at the end of every sentence.

You're being clear. You're being efficient. You're being someone people actually listen to—**because you sound like you listen to yourself.**

First Impressions Aren't Just Visual—They're Sensory

You walk into a room—maybe a boardroom, maybe a first date, maybe your in-laws' house, and before you even say hello, something has already happened. People have made a call on you. Not a conscious, spreadsheet-level call. A *body-level call.* A feeling. A vibe. A "this person has their shit together" or "this person feels a little all over the place" or "this person is clearly fighting with their jacket right now and might cry if I ask them how they're doing."

And here's the kicker: most of that first impression? It has absolutely *nothing* to do with how you look.

Not your outfit. Not your haircut. Not even your body language in the traditional "hands out of your pockets, shoulders back" sense. It's **your presence**. Your *energy.* The emotional texture you carry into the room like a scent that hits before you've said a single damn word.

It's sensory. People don't see it. They *feel* it.

Which is why someone can walk into a room in an old T-shirt and command it without raising their voice. And someone else can be in head-to-toe designer power couture and still feel like they're apologizing for being there.

Because it's not about polish. It's about **weight.**

Weight = energetic credibility

You know that feeling when someone starts speaking and everyone stops fidgeting, puts down their phone, and actually listens? That's weight.

You also know that feeling when someone walks in, starts speaking, and immediately gets talked over, ignored, or nodded at politely while everyone's already checked out? That's a lack of weight. Even if they're saying something smart. Even if they're technically qualified.

Here's the brutal truth: if people aren't feeling you, they're not hearing you.

And if they're not hearing you, your message dies before it ever gets a chance to matter.

So, what gives someone that kind of presence?

It's not posture alone. Though posture helps.

It's not eye contact alone. Though eye contact matters.

It's the **full-body vibe** that says:

- I'm grounded.
- I'm not rushing.
- I'm not trying to prove anything.
- I believe what I'm saying before you even need to.

That's it. That's the secret. And it's maddeningly simple and ridiculously hard to fake.

How do you create that kind of sensory presence?

You start before you speak.

You ground. You breathe. You remember what room you're in and what version of yourself you actually want to bring to the table. Not the defensive one. Not the performative one. The **steady** one. The one that doesn't care if people are judging your delivery because you're too busy being present with your message.

And then you enter. Fully. Not just physically. Mentally. Emotionally. Shoulders open. Chin level. Not exaggerated like some corporate robot on a TEDx stage, but just *there.* No flinching. No fidgeting. No rehearsed swagger. Just that quiet, unbothered energy of someone who knows they deserve to be in the room because **they're already in the room.**

And what about facial expressions?

Oh, I'm so glad you asked. Because some of y'all are out here giving accidental murder vibes without meaning to. Or the opposite—smiling so hard your jaw cramps because you don't want to come off "intense."

Here's the rule: **your face is a headline.** And the reader is the room.

If you look guarded, rushed, distracted, or vaguely resentful (hi RBF, I see you), people will read that before they read your words. If you look curious, engaged, grounded—even neutral but awake—people will lean in. Because they trust what they *feel* more than what they hear.

So, **train your face to match your intention.** Not to perform. Not to manipulate. Just to align.

Your resting face doesn't have to look like a stock photo. But it does have to say: "I'm here. I'm listening. And I'm not two seconds from emotionally exiting this conversation."

That alone will elevate every room you walk into.

The moment you enter is your message before your message

Every time you open a door, join a call, walk onstage, or even hit "unmute," your presence has already started speaking. Not in words. In *sensation.* In the way people feel in their bodies when they're around you.

It says, "This person is safe." Or "This person's hiding something." Or "This person is about to emotionally collapse if you ask them to repeat that last point."

So, give people the message you *actually* want to send.

And here's the best part: you don't have to fake it. You just have to **get present.** People aren't looking for you to be perfect. They're just looking for a signal—any signal—that says, *"You're not about to waste their time, flinch mid-sentence, or spiral halfway through the meeting."*

And if you can send that signal with your face, your tone, your pause, your silence—before you even get to the point? That's the real mic drop.

Energy Before Delivery

You ever say something perfectly reasonable, well-worded, even kind of brilliant, and it still lands flat? Or worse, it gets ignored entirely, as if your voice came with a mute button and everyone pressed it in unison?

That's not because your point sucked. It's not because you didn't try. It's because your *energy* was off.

Not in a woo-woo, "align your chakras and burn sage before the Zoom call" kind of way (unless you're into that, in which case, bless). I mean in the very real, very physical sense that people don't just hear you—they *feel you.* They can smell your panic, your people-pleasing, your inner chaos. They read the microtension in your jaw and shoulders. They notice your tone before they register your message. And they are responding to *that.*

Before you even speak, you're already communicating. The question is: what are you saying?

Because if you're carrying the energy of **"Please don't hate me,"** or **"I hope this is okay,"** or **"I'm trying really hard to sound smart right now,"** guess what? People will feel it. And that little static in your nervous system will muddy every word that follows.

So, how do you fix your energy before you speak?

First, you stop thinking the solution is in your script.

It's not about saying the exact right thing. It's about the **state you're in when you say it.** Think about athletes. Or actors. Or even great public speakers. They don't just rehearse words. They rehearse **state**. Calm. Focused. Locked in. They know that if their nervous system is shot, their message won't land.

Same goes for you.

You don't need to prep another bullet point. You need to **get inside your body.**

Ground your feet. Breathe like a person who doesn't hate themselves.

Unclench your jaw. (Yes, it's clenched right now. Unclench it.)

Put your phone down. Close the 12 mental tabs you have open about what you're supposed to say, how you're supposed to say it, and what they'll think of you if you screw it up.

That moment before you speak? **That's where presence is born.**

Grounding is not a vibe—it's a tactic

This is not about being "chill." It's about being *available to yourself* so you're not white-knuckling through the sentence hoping to sound polished while your soul screams into a pillow.

Try this before a hard conversation:

- Put both feet flat on the floor.
- Drop your attention to your legs. Feel their weight.

- Breathe in for four, hold for four, breathe out for six. (Yes, it matters.)
- Say—out loud if you can—"I'm allowed to take up space."
- Then speak.

And if you're in public and feel weird doing that out loud? Fine. Say it in your head. No one has to know you're regulating your inner chaos like a seasoned hostage negotiator.

Don't try to *calm down.* Try to *slow down.*

"Calm down" is bullshit advice. It's vague. Patronizing. And usually delivered by someone who is either not nervous at all or deeply annoying.

Instead, try to **slow** down. Slow your speech. Slow your breath. Slow your movements. It signals to your body, and to the room—that you are not in danger. And when you stop behaving like you're in danger, people stop treating you like you're unstable.

Confidence doesn't feel like excitement. It feels like **steadiness**.

Say less, better

When you're nervous, the urge to overtalk is real. You want to fill the silence, preempt their questions, clarify everything you *might* get wrong. You word-vomit for the sake of control, but the only thing you're controlling is how quickly people check out.

So, don't aim for perfect. Aim for **clear**. And clear requires space. Let the pause do the heavy lifting. Let your sentence breathe. Don't rush to patch every quiet second with more talking—it just waters down your message.

Say the thing. Let it sit. Breathe.

Then say the next thing.

That's presence. That's weight. That's what authority *sounds* like.

You are not your nerves

Last thing: just because you feel nervous doesn't mean you're being perceived as weak. Most of the time, people can't tell unless you tell them. And even if they *can* sense it—they're probably too busy managing their own performance anxiety to give a shit.

So, stop letting your inner monologue narrate the whole experience like a courtroom drama. Your energy doesn't need to be perfect. It just needs to be **yours**. Aligned. Real. A little shaky? Fine. **But grounded in something deeper than the need to perform.**

When people hear that kind of energy—that unbothered, not-here-to-beg-for-validation tone—they don't just listen. **They lean in.**

And isn't that the whole point?

Speak With Weight (Even When You're New, Nervous, or Outranked)

There's a very specific kind of internal spiral that kicks in when you're about to speak and the room is stacked with people who make more money than you, have fancier titles, carry more confidence, or radiate that terrifying calm that only comes from knowing they've done this a hundred times before.

You feel it coming. That tiny panic. That tightness in your throat. That desire to shrink just a little, be agreeable, keep your point short, maybe even let it go entirely because "who am I to say anything?" But here's the thing: if you only ever speak when you feel powerful, you'll barely speak at all. Because in the rooms that matter most, you'll almost *always* be the newest, youngest, least established, or most out-of-place person at some point. That's not a glitch. That's the assignment.

So, what do you do?

You stop trying to **sound** powerful.

And you start learning how to **speak with weight.**

Weight ≠ volume, posture, or fake swagger

We already ditched those earlier in the chapter. You know by now that loud doesn't equal strong, and polished doesn't mean respected.

Weight is something else. It's **gravitas.** Not because you're older or more experienced, but because you've decided to treat your words like they matter, even when no one's handed you the microphone.

And that means:

- You don't defer *just* because someone has a title.
- You don't preface your points with, "I know I'm still new…"
- You don't ask for space. You *take* it—calmly, respectfully, like it was already yours.

Because guess what? It is.

Power is often handed to the person who sounds most comfortable holding it

Not the one who has the best idea.

Not the one who's been there the longest.

Not the one with the fanciest credentials.

The one who makes other people feel like, *"Okay. This person's solid. They're not flailing. I can exhale while they talk."*

That doesn't mean being slick. It doesn't mean rehearsed. It means grounded delivery, sure, but it also means knowing how to *enter the conversation without collapsing into apology or permission-seeking mode.*

Even when you're shitless scared, even when the table is full of executives or even when you're thinking, "I don't belong here."

Because in that moment, **how you see yourself** leaks through every word. And you can either let that be a quiet act of self-doubt—or a quiet act of self-claiming.

So, how do you speak with weight in those moments?

Not by flexing. Not by listing your credentials mid-sentence or talking like a human résumé.

You do it by:

- **Speaking last** when you can. Not to delay, but to assess. People who observe first and speak second naturally command attention.
- **Owning the damn silence.** Say your point. Let it land. Don't fill the space. Trust that the weight will do the talking.
- **Holding eye contact with one person.** Not the whole room. Just one person at a time. Like you're not performing. You're *connecting.*
- **Choosing words that cut the fluff.** No maybes, no over-explaining. "What I'm seeing is this." "Here's what's getting missed." "This is what I recommend." Period. Done.

What about when you get interrupted?

It's going to happen. Especially if you're younger, female, quieter, or perceived as junior. Some dude named Greg with an inflated LinkedIn profile and a chronic interrupting habit is probably going to cut you off mid-thought.

Here's what you do:

- **Pause. Look at him. Then say, without rushing:**
- "I wasn't finished."
- Or, "Hang on, let me wrap that thought."
- Or if you want to stay elegant but steel-tipped:
- "Just let me land that, then I'll hand it over."

You don't need to escalate. Just **reclaim the floor like you never lost it**. And then continue like it never happened. Power isn't in the snark, it's in the *non-reactivity*. The casual reset. The refusal to shrink.

Speaking with weight isn't about being the expert. It's about being *anchored.*

You don't have to be the smartest person in the room. You just have to be the one who **believes their point enough to say it without flinching**.

That's what people remember.

They don't walk away quoting your exact words. They walk away thinking, *"Damn. She was solid. She meant it."*

And in a world of noise, flailing, and overtalking, that kind of quiet steadiness is magnetic.

So, if you're new? Fine. Own it. But don't you dare use it as a reason to make yourself small.

If you're nervous? Good. That means you care. But don't let that care turn into self-erasure.

If you're outranked? That's just optics. Presence doesn't show up on an org chart. Speak like your words matter. Say what needs saying. And don't rush to end the moment just because it's uncomfortable.

Because if you can hold that discomfort and still *land the point*?

You just became the most powerful voice in the room.

When You Can't Find Your Moment to Speak

This one's personal. Because I still struggle with it.

Not every time. Not in every room. But often enough that I know the pattern. I've sat in meetings where I had something smart, important, even potentially game-changing to say, but by the time I opened my mouth, someone else was already mid-sentence, the conversation had moved on, or worse, my point suddenly felt like dead weight. Irrelevant. Out of place. Too late.

So, I didn't say it.

And then I left the meeting frustrated. Not with them—with *myself.*

Because I'd talked myself out of my own moment… again.

If you know that feeling—of waiting, watching, holding your idea like a delicate little balloon while the room swells with louder voices until there's no space left for yours—I want to tell you: **you're not alone.** And no, you're not weak, or slow, or "not cut out" for high-pressure conversations. You've just been trained—by culture, by school, by experience—to **wait your turn.**

But turns don't always come.

And if you keep waiting for one, you'll keep leaving rooms unheard.

Reclaim Your Power: Speak Before You're Ready

You don't need to wait for the perfect pause. You don't need everyone's eyes on you or a smooth little gap in the conversation where you're "allowed" to slide in. That moment—the one you keep hoping for? Half the room isn't waiting for it. They're just talking. Loudly. Confidently. Often about nothing.

So, stop waiting to be invited. Interrupt if you need to. Raise your hand. Clear your throat. Cut in.

Because your voice deserves space *now*—not later. Not when it's safe. Not when it's polished. Now.

This doesn't mean being rude. It means being done with shrinking. With second-guessing. With handing the floor over again and again because you're worried your timing isn't perfect or your sentence isn't fully formed.

Power isn't polite. It's *present*. Speak before you're ready. You'll survive it. And your voice? It might just be the thing that changes the whole damn room.

You're not lacking confidence—you're playing by rules that don't exist

Somewhere along the line, you learned that the respectful thing to do is wait for the right moment. For the pause. The perfect opening. The clear invitation to speak. But in most rooms—especially high-pressure, fast-paced, opinion-heavy ones—those pauses are rare and that invitation? Nonexistent.

The people who get heard aren't always the smartest. They're just the ones who've made peace with being **slightly interruptive**. With not waiting for permission. With cutting in—cleanly, clearly, and without apology.

And I get it. That feels uncomfortable. I still get that surge of "Oh god, am I being rude?" every time I interrupt someone. But let me tell you what's actually rude: **the world never hearing your ideas because you were too polite to claim space.**

Let's break it down—what's actually happening in those moments?

You're listening—*intently*, probably better than anyone else in the room. You're building your point in real time. You want to respond thoughtfully, not just talk for the sake of it. You're waiting for the lull.

But the lull keeps getting swallowed. By someone louder. Or faster. Or less hesitant to throw their thought out half-baked and see what sticks.

Meanwhile, you're still trying to get your wording just right. Still checking if it's the right time. Still thinking, *Do I even need to say this anymore? Is it still relevant?*

And then it's gone. And you're left with a brilliant point and nowhere to put it. Again.

Here's what I've learned (and what I'm still learning)

1. **You don't need a perfect opening—you just need to *mark the space***
2. Don't wait until you've mentally rehearsed your whole point before jumping in.
3. **Just say:**
    - "Before we shift gears—can I add something here?"
    - "I'd like to build on that point…"
    - "Hang on, I'd like to speak to that."

That's all. That's the doorway. Say that first. Then breathe. *Then* speak.

4. **You don't owe anyone flawless timing—only presence**
5. If someone else jumps in and takes the moment before you can? Fine. Let them speak. And then calmly say:
6. "When you're done, I'd still like to share what I was going to add a moment ago."
7. Simple. No apology. No drama. No shrinking. Just a gentle reset.
8. **Bring your voice back, even if the conversation moved on**
9. This one's hard, but powerful. If your point still matters—even if the group has zigzagged off course—*bring it back.*
10. **Try:**

  - "I know we've moved on, but earlier there was something I didn't want to leave unsaid…"
  - "I wanted to circle back quickly to what we discussed a few minutes ago—because I think there's a gap we might've missed."

If you don't bring it back, no one will know it was missing.

11. **Your silence is not neutral**
12. It *feels* like the safe option in the moment. But over time, it **costs you.**
13. You miss chances. You reinforce the idea that your voice isn't a priority. And—maybe worst of all—you start to believe it.

So, even when you're nervous. Even when your timing's messy. Even when the moment doesn't feel perfect—**Take. The. Space.**

One final thing, from one late-speaker to another:

There is nothing wrong with the way you think, there is nothing wrong with how carefully you listen, and there is nothing wrong with wanting to be respectful, clear, and measured.

But when that caution becomes a muzzle?

When it becomes the reason you leave meetings unheard, conversations unfinished, opportunities unclaimed?

Then it's time to interrupt.

Not rudely. Not aggressively. But *deliberately.*

You can speak with grace *and* impact.

You can take up space *without apologizing.*

And you can stop waiting for permission to say the thing that matters.

Because no one's going to hand you the mic.

But I promise—you're allowed to take it.

You don't need louder words. You need to believe the quieter ones still count.

You don't need perfect timing. You need to stop waiting for an invitation that's never coming.

Because confidence isn't about taking over the room—it's about refusing to disappear from it.

You've learned how to sound solid, speak clearly, and show up with presence. Now comes the real test: **Can you hold your voice when it's uncomfortable? Can you protect your time, your energy, your boundaries, without folding, flinching, or lighting yourself on fire to keep the peace?**

If Chapter 4 helped you *own the room*, Chapter 5 will help you *own yourself in it.*

Let's go.

Be the Reason Someone Gets Heard Today

Hey you :)

Yes —*you*, the one who actually reads the back-matter instead of immediately hunting for the QR code. (I like you already. You're my people.)

If this book made you laugh, think, breathe easier, or finally understand why your texts get misread, your boundaries get bulldozed, or your brilliant ideas die in meetings — you can pay it forward in one ridiculously simple way:

Leave a review.

That's it.

One sentence like:

- "I finally stopped getting talked over."
- "This book saved me from rage-replying to a dry 'k.'"
- "Apparently, I wasn't the problem. My communication habits were."

Reviews help other adults — the overwhelmed, the overthinkers, the quiet ones, the loud ones, the ones stuck in conflict — find this book right when they need it.

It takes 30 seconds.

It changes everything for an indie author.

And yes… it might stop a full-grown adult from sending a 14-paragraph email nobody asked for.

Scan the first QR code below to leave your review and officially become the reason someone else finally learns how to communicate like a functioning human.

(Cape optional. Confidence mandatory.)

Curious What Else I Wrote?

Turns out one book doesn't fix a whole life. (Believe me, I tried.)

Scan the second QR code to see the rest of the collection. Same voice. Same no-BS approach. Different flavours of the same underlying idea: you're not broken, you've just been handed bad advice by people trying to sell you something shinier than the truth.

Whatever's chewing on you right now — a relationship that's turned into unpaid emotional labour, money that disappears before you understand where it went, a brain that won't stop rehearsing arguments at 2am, or (yes) a garden bed that refuses to grow anything but weeds — there's probably a book for it.

Pick the one that hits closest.

No spam. No motivational speeches at 6 a.m. Just books, occasional updates, and the kind of tools your therapist would give you if she wasn't watching the clock.

One Last Thing

Actually, One More Thing

If any of this landed — if you saw yourself in the overexplainer, the overthinker, the one carrying the emotional weight of every room she walks into — there's a book you probably need more than this one.

You're Not His Therapist.

For women who keep ending up as the translator, the peacekeeper, the one running the whole conversation while he grunts at his phone.

Same voice. Same no-BS toolkit. Different problem, same underlying pattern of doing all the heavy lifting in a relationship you didn't sign up to run.

If Communication Skills gave you the words, *You're Not His Therapist* tells you when to stop wasting them on someone who isn't listening.

Scan to grab a copy. Or don't.

CHAPTER 5:

Boundaries Aren't Rude—They're Expensive Energy Management

Because You Can't Keep Having Conversations That Suck the Life Out of You

Not Everyone Deserves a Front-Row Seat to Your Energy

I'd like to get something uncomfortable out of the way from the get-go—because this is the one that took me way too long to learn, and even longer to actually apply without backpedaling or spiraling afterward: just because someone wants your attention, doesn't mean they deserve your energy. Just because they have access to you—via a phone, a hallway, a shared Slack channel, a long-standing relationship, or their general presence in your life—doesn't automatically mean they're entitled to an audience, a response, or your emotional bandwidth in that moment.

And I say that not with judgment, but with a deep sigh of exhaustion—because I've been the person who gives out front-row passes like candy, who takes every message, every "hey, quick thing," every emotional download or unfiltered vent as something I need to be present for, respond to, help solve, or at least not walk away from. I thought it made me kind. Compassionate. Supportive. Empathetic. What it actually made me was chronically drained, quietly resentful, and somehow never fully available to the people or priorities that **actually mattered** to me—because I was so damn busy trying to be emotionally available to everyone else.

And if that hits? You're not alone. Especially if you've been conditioned—by upbringing, culture, work, or just years of being the "good listener"—to think that saying no makes you cold, or unavailable, or worse, selfish.

But here's something you should know: **your energy isn't a public utility**. You don't **owe** it to everyone. You get to choose where it goes.

And if you don't, someone else will choose for you. Probably loudly. Probably often.

There's this unspoken script so many of us carry around, where we equate being emotionally open with being emotionally *accessible*. We think compassion means always being on call. That generosity means never saying "not today." That if someone shows up with their pain, or their drama, or their never-ending need for validation dressed up as conversation, it's our job to sit down, open our ears, and hold space—even if we're hanging on by a thread ourselves.

But that's not generosity. That's erosion.

Because when your compassion is on tap 24/7, and you never filter who gets to drink from it, you stop having anything left for the things you actually **want** to be generous with. The people who light you up. The projects that need your full attention. The rest and solitude that refill you enough to keep showing up at all.

And I get it—this isn't an easy shift. Especially when you've built an identity around being "the one who's always there." Saying "no" feels mean. Saying "not now" feels dismissive. And saying nothing at all feels like abandonment.

But here's what's actually happening when you constantly offer yourself up as a landing pad for other people's chaos: you're teaching them that your time doesn't need to be considered, your energy doesn't need to be earned, and your boundaries are more of a vague suggestion than an actual guideline.

And people, bless them, will **take** what you keep giving.

It doesn't mean they're manipulative. Most of them probably don't even realize they're draining you. But if you've never said, "I don't have the capacity for this right now," how would they know? If you've never paused the conversation and said, "Can we come back to this another time? I need to ground myself first," how would they learn that you *have* a limit?

They won't. Not until you show them.

And yes, the first time you say it, it might land weird. You might fumble the words. You might feel guilty, or over-explain, or apologize ten times before and after just to make sure they still like you. That's fine. That's part of the work. We're not aiming for smooth—we're aiming for **true**.

Because it's better to say "not now" and be present later than to nod your way through a conversation that makes your chest feel tight and your brain feel like a browser with 47 tabs open, none of which are relevant and all of which are slowing you down.

This is not about cutting people out. It's about **being conscious of who's getting access to your emotional bandwidth and why**. It's about remembering that your attention is a gift, not an obligation. It's about choosing when to open the front row and when to close the damn curtains because the show is over for today and you need to sit backstage with snacks and silence.

Not everyone gets your full presence. Not everyone gets to dump their emotional junk on your metaphorical porch and expect you to sort through it with a flashlight and a snack tray. And not everyone needs to understand your boundaries in order for them to still be valid.

You're allowed to choose how and when you show up. You're allowed to say, "Not today." You're allowed to close the door—even if someone's knocking.

Because your energy? It's sacred. And it's time you started treating it that way.

When You've Taught Them to Expect Too Much (and You Want Out Without Burning It Down)

Sometimes, the reason your energy is being taken for granted isn't because people are selfish—it's because **you taught them that access to you would always be unlimited**. You didn't mean to. You just kept showing up. You kept saying yes. You made space even when you didn't have it. You wanted to be generous, supportive, kind, and maybe, if we're being brutally honest, needed. So, you kept giving until "giving" wasn't a choice anymore, it was a *pattern.*

And now that pattern is strangling you.

Maybe you've realized it slowly—like a relationship that used to feel good but now just feels like a job you didn't apply for. Or maybe it hit you all at once, that sharp, breathless moment where you realized you can't do it anymore. Not like this. Not with this imbalance. Not with this weight.

So, what do you do when you've already built the dynamic and now want to change the terms, without setting the whole thing on fire?

You **retrain the relationship**. Not with a dramatic confrontation or a friendship breakup or a long, emotionally exhausting debrief (though sure, if that's your style, go for it). You start quietly. Consistently. Firmly. You stop overfunctioning. You stop rewarding entitlement. You stop pretending that what you're giving doesn't cost you anything.

And yeah—it's awkward. It's clumsy. It might piss people off. But if the relationship is solid underneath, it'll survive the recalibration. If it's not? Then it wasn't really a relationship. It was a transaction you were subsidizing with your silence.

You don't owe anyone access just because they got used to having it.

You don't need to justify pulling back when you've been the one holding it all up. And you're not cruel for deciding your energy is no longer up for grabs.

You're just **done being the one who keeps paying for the connection with parts of yourself you never meant to give away.**

And let's be honest—it *feels* like you'll have to blow it up just to breathe again.

But you don't.

Here's what you do instead:

First, get honest—with yourself, not them (yet)

Before you say a word to the other person, you have to name the real problem. And no, it's not just "they take too much." The real problem is: **you taught them to**. Not maliciously. Not consciously. But consistently.

You've reinforced the behavior. You've trained them that you'll always show up, that your "no" is soft and reversible, that you'll stretch even when it hurts. You gave the crumbs permission to be enough. And now they think they're feeding you.

It's okay. You're not weak. You're human. You wanted connection. You thought this was the way to keep it. But now you're allowed to want something different.

Then, set the new baseline—*quietly, consistently, and without making it a dramatic event*

You don't need a manifesto. You don't need to corner them with a speech about how taken-for-granted you feel.

But what often works better is recalibration in motion.

Start saying no—*gently*, but firmly. Start taking longer to reply.

Start declining last-minute calls or emotional downloads with, "Hey, I'm not up for this today." Stop over-explaining. Stop cushioning every boundary with guilt. Stop offering 17 alternatives when you say you're not available.

And most importantly: **don't flinch when they notice the change.**

Because they will. Especially if they've come to rely on you being the one who always gives more than you get.

What if they get upset?

Here's the part that hurts, but frees you:

Their discomfort doesn't mean you're doing something wrong. It just means you've changed the rules, and they were benefiting from the old ones.

If the relationship is healthy at its core, they'll adjust. They might stumble, push back a little, or ask what's going on. That's okay. You can say:

- "I realized I've been overextending myself, and I'm trying to be more intentional about where my energy goes."
- "I love you and I want to stay connected, but I need to rebalance how I've been showing up."
- "I've noticed I've been burning out, and I'm working on not ignoring my own needs. So, I might not always be as available as I've been in the past."

Not angry. Not accusatory. Just clear. Real. Grounded in self-respect, not revenge.

What if they don't adjust?

This is the heartbreak territory. The part where you learn that some relationships are only functional when you're over-functioning. Where they don't actually know how to relate to you without taking. Where your self-abandonment was the glue holding things together.

And when you stop offering yourself up on the altar of being liked, or loved, or needed, or indispensable, the relationship might crack.

Let it.

Because staying in a dynamic that feeds on your silence isn't kindness. It's codependence dressed up as loyalty.

You deserve to have relationships where your **boundaries aren't seen as threats**, but as *proof that you trust the connection to withstand honesty.*

Slow withdrawal is still withdrawal. It's okay to grieve.

There's something incredibly lonely about shifting a long-standing dynamic. You might feel guilty. Ungrateful. Even cruel. But please hear this:

Protecting your peace does not make you the villain. Reclaiming your energy is not betrayal. Choosing yourself is not the same as rejecting them.

You are not abandoning the relationship. You are just ending the part of it that required you to abandon *yourself.*

Because here's what finally broke it open for me—what I couldn't unsee once it landed: **The more I gave, the less I got in return.** And not because they were trying to hurt me, but because I made it *too easy not to give anything back.*

That's when I realized this wasn't generosity. It was depletion disguised as connection. And I had to stop feeding a system that kept rewarding my silence.

Graceful Exits — How to Step Back Without Ghosting or Guilt-Tripping Yourself

So, now you see it clearly: you've overgiven, overfunctioned, and overextended. You've realized you've trained people to treat your energy like it's always available on demand. And you've made the call: *I need to step back.*

But here comes the next problem: **How the hell do you do that without ghosting, imploding the relationship, or turning into a guilt-ridden mess who texts "sorry!! just been so slammed" every three days while still resenting every word?**

This is where most people get stuck.

You don't want to ghost. You don't want to lie. You don't want to make it a big emotional announcement. And you sure as hell don't want to reopen the vault by overexplaining, backpedaling, or asking for permission to take a break from being everyone's emotional Swiss Army knife.

What you want is a *clean, kind, steady exit strategy*—one that lets you protect your bandwidth **without punishing the other person or betraying yourself.**

So, let's talk strategy.

---

1. Use clear language, not vague dodges

There's nothing worse than the emotional slow fade—those text replies that keep getting shorter, the "sorry just flat out!" messages that start to feel more like a brush-off than the truth. If you want to maintain integrity in the relationship, even while stepping back, you need to **say what's true without turning it into a drama.**

Here's what that looks like:

"Hey, I want to be real with you—my capacity has been stretched lately, and I'm trying to protect my energy a little more. I might not be as available as I've been before, but I care about you and I hope you'll understand."

"I've realized I've been overcommitting myself emotionally, and I'm working on pulling back where I need to. That includes being slower to respond or needing more space, but it's not personal."

You're not apologizing. You're **informing**. You're not ghosting. You're **resetting the terms**.

If the person respects you, they'll get it. If they don't? That's useful data too.

---

2. Script your way through the awkward middle

You're going to feel weird the first few times you say it. That's fine. You can prepare for that with what I call the **two-step soft exit**.

Here's how it works:

- **Step 1**: Acknowledge the connection
- **Step 2**: Name your boundary clearly, without apology

Example:

"I always appreciate how open you are with me. I've just been noticing that I'm emotionally overloaded lately, so I may need to take more space and be more intentional about when I engage."

That's it. You don't owe them a reason *why*. You don't need to prove how burnt out you are. You're stating a new limit—not applying for a hall pass.

---

3. Don't be afraid to close the door gently

Not every exit needs to be open-ended. If someone's been emotionally dependent on you in a way that doesn't feel mutual, or if you know the dynamic isn't healthy, it's okay to step away with clarity.

Try:

"I want to be honest with you—this dynamic has been leaving me feeling drained, and I need to take a step back for my own mental space. I don't expect anything from you, I just wanted to be clear rather than disappear."

Notice the tone: **not defensive, not aggressive, not blaming**. Just *clear and calm.*

You're not slamming the door. You're *closing it with the grace they didn't give you when they walked in uninvited.*

---

4. Expect guilt, but don't confuse it with wrongdoing

That little pang you'll feel after you hit send or walk away? That's not a sign you did something wrong. It's just a signal that you're doing something *different.* And difference often registers as danger to a nervous system that's been trained to keep the peace at all costs.

So, breathe through the guilt. Let it exist. Then let it pass.

Remind yourself:

- You're not cutting people off—you're *cutting yourself loose from a role you never agreed to.*
- You're not being selfish—you're *making sure there's something left of you to show up for the right people.*
- You're not ghosting—you're *protecting your peace with words instead of withdrawal.*

That's growth. It's uncomfortable. And it's absolutely necessary.

---

5. What if they guilt you? What if they're hurt?

Then they're showing you how little space they've made for your humanity in the relationship.

If someone can only value you when you're endlessly available, if they only see you as generous when you say yes, if they're wounded by your absence but indifferent to your exhaustion—*that is not a relationship, that's a service agreement.*

You're allowed to change the terms.

And if they lash out? Let that be the proof you needed. Because someone who loves you won't punish you for protecting yourself.

They'll adjust.

Final note:

You don't have to pull back perfectly. You don't have to script every boundary in advance. You don't have to avoid every awkward silence, every misunderstood pause, every shift in tone that makes you wonder if they're mad at you.

You just have to start showing up like your energy is worth protecting.

Because it is.

And if they can't meet you in that space? You'll be okay. Because you finally are.

The Power of a Hard Stop

Because Sometimes the Kindest Thing You Can Do—for Everyone Involved—is Stop Talking

Let's just say it: conversations that drag on forever, that keep looping or spiraling or testing your ability to stay awake without blinking too much, are exhausting. Not just because they're long, but because they don't know where the edge is. There's no off-ramp. No limit. No *container.* You start off with good intentions and then suddenly it's an hour later, you've nodded 300 times, and your brain is now begging you to chew your own arm off to escape politely.

This is where the **hard stop** comes in—not as some harsh shutdown or cold boundary drop, but as a way of protecting the time and energy you need to stay present *without* burning out or having to fake a weak phone signal just to get out of a conversation.

And no, it doesn't make you rude. It makes you clear. Which, let's be honest, is what most people actually need more of, not less.

Why we struggle to do it

Somewhere along the line, a lot of us got the idea that once a conversation starts, we're not allowed to be the one who ends it. Like we signed a verbal lease and we're locked in for the duration, no matter how much the topic shifts, how many times we say "anyway," or how badly we need to pee, cry, or eat a snack in silence.

But that's not communication. That's **emotional hostage-taking** with a polite smile.

So, here's the truth bomb you might need to hear:

You're allowed to leave.

Even if the other person hasn't stopped talking.

Even if you feel like you should stay just five more minutes.

Even if you're afraid of seeming rude or uninterested or unkind.

Even if it's your boss. Even if it's your mother. Even if it's your best friend in the middle of a crisis.

Because staying when you're spent doesn't make you kind—it makes you resentful. And people can feel that, even if they don't know what to call it.

So, what does a hard stop actually look like?

It's not a script. It's not a confrontation. It's not you storming out of the Zoom room mid-sentence. It's you **letting the other person know where your line is—before you cross it.**

Like this:

- *"I've got about fifteen minutes before I need to shift gears, but I'd love to hear what's going on."*
- *"I can talk now, but I need to jump off at three sharp."*

- *"Just a heads-up, I'm not at full capacity today, so I'll probably keep it short."*

What you're doing here is offering presence **within limits**.

And honestly? That's a gift.

Because no one can be fully present forever. Not even with people we love.

People actually like it more than you think

You know what happens when you give a conversation structure?

It **relieves pressure** on both sides.

It helps the other person focus.

It shows that you're someone who values your time, and by extension, **theirs**.

And most of the time, they appreciate it—even if they don't say so out loud. They feel it. It feels safe. Like you know how to hold space *without falling into it.*

And if they don't like it? If they huff or push or try to guilt you into "just one more thing"? That tells you something. Because someone who needs you to never leave the conversation probably isn't really having a conversation. They're having a monologue with a captive audience.

You're not an audience. You're a person. With edges. With needs. With a schedule. With a brain that needs time to rest and reset and not process everyone's words like a personal Google Doc for emotional labor.

If you don't set the boundary, you'll keep paying for it later

You'll pay for it in the irritation you don't express.

You'll pay for it in the exhaustion that leaks into other conversations you actually care about.

You'll pay for it in the passive-aggressive mood shift that happens when someone keeps talking and you're five miles past done but too "nice" to say so.

So, let's stop pretending this is just about being polite.

This is about energy management.

This is about showing up fully **and** knowing when to step out.

This is about building conversations that have a middle **and** an end—so you don't start resenting the people you actually care about just because you forgot how to say, *"That's all I've got for today."*

Want a super simple rule?

If you're entering a conversation and you already know you've got limited time or energy, **say so up front.** Not later. Not after the fourth "yeah, totally." Not once you're halfway dissociated. At the beginning.

And then—this is important—**actually honor it.** Leave when you said you would. Don't waffle. Don't apologize. Just wrap it up like the adult you are.

"Okay, I'm going to pause us here—I need to switch gears. Thanks for catching up."

"I'm out of steam, so I'm going to head off for now, but let's pick this up another time if we need to."

Short. Kind. Clean. You're not disappearing. You're just *done.*

Here's the secret:

A hard stop isn't about pushing people away.
It's about making sure you can actually stay connected, **without becoming a shadow of yourself in the process.**

And if someone takes your boundary personally? You can breathe through it, smile if you feel like it, and remind yourself that your time is not up for debate. Because people who love you, respect you, or even just function like decent humans **will adapt.**

And the ones who don't?

Well, now you know where you actually stand.

CHAPTER 6:

Digital Communication Without the Cringe Factor

Texting 'k' can ruin friendships faster than spilling red wine on white carpet.

Emails That Get Replies Instead of Eye Rolls

Let's start with the digital dinosaur of 'em all: email.

Email isn't dead. It's just become the office equivalent of background noise—everyone hears it, no one listens to it, and half of us are secretly hoping the email we just sent gets ignored because we're already spiraling about whether it made sense.

But if you want your emails to *actually* get read, and replied to—you need to treat them less like a formal letter from the 1800s and more like a clear, well-placed nudge that respects people's time and energy. And no, that doesn't mean skipping punctuation or writing like a Slack bot with heat-stroke. It means **sounding human**, while still getting to the point.

Here's how.

---

1. Nail the subject line

The subject line is not an afterthought—it's the *billboard* for your message. If it sounds vague, corporate, or like spam, it's going in the mental trash can.

Bad:

- "Touching base"
- "Quick check-in"
- "Follow-up from earlier"

Better:

- "Need your approval by Friday: Budget line 3"
- "Update: Workshop outline ready for review"
- "Schedule request: 15 mins this week?"

Clear. Specific. Action-oriented. If your subject line could be slapped on any random email from your inbox, it's not doing its job.

---

2. Skip the passive voice and faux-politeness

"I just wanted to reach out…" "I was hoping to possibly…"

"I realize you're super busy…"

You think you're being thoughtful. But you're actually burying the ask.

Be polite, not apologetic. You can be direct and still sound like a decent human.

Try this:

- "Can you take a look at this by EOD?"
- "Is Tuesday or Thursday better for you?"
- "Attaching the revised deck—let me know if you want edits."

Clarity reads as respect. Word salad reads as anxiety.

---

3. Use the sandwich method, but make it real

Not every email needs to start with fake cheer ("Happy Friday!") or a line that's clearly just small talk camouflage. But starting with a little warmth goes a long way, especially if the body of the email involves feedback, deadlines, or any tone that could be misread as "abrupt."

The sandwich method = start soft, deliver the point, end warm.

Example:

Hey Sam,

Loved how you opened the client call today—it really set the tone.

I've flagged a couple of follow-ups in the doc (attached) that need your review before Friday.

Let me know if you want to chat through them. Thanks again for jumping in.

You're not fluffing. You're setting emotional context, without wasting time.

---

4. Get in, get out

The perfect email is like a clean landing in gymnastics. No wobble. No ramble. One clear point per paragraph. Short sentences. Clear ask. Brief context. Done.

If your email is longer than a phone screen and doesn't include a bulleted list or subhead, rethink it. People don't read emails. They scan them. So, structure your message like you're doing them a favor—which you are.

Try This: The One-Minute Email Audit

Before you hit send, ask yourself:

- **Is the subject line specific?**
- **Did I say what I want clearly and early?**
- **Is there one action item—not five?**
- **Does the tone sound like me on a normal, well-slept day?**
- **Could someone reply with a single sentence? If not, did I ask too many things at once?**

If you nailed all five, congrats. Your email might actually get answered.

Texting Without the Drama

Texting shouldn't feel like emotional landmine navigation. And yet… here we are. One-word replies. Ambiguous emojis. That eerie silence when you see they've "read" your message and then just... *didn't respond.*

Welcome to modern communication, where the words you type are only half the message, and the other half is a mix of tone, timing, and psychic guesswork.

So, if you've ever agonized over how many dots to put in your ellipsis or rewritten "no worries at all!" six different ways because you weren't sure if it sounded passive-aggressive… this section is for you.

---

1. One-word replies are a vibe, and not a good one

You may think a quick "yep" or "fine" is efficient. But in texting, it doesn't read as "clear and to the point." It reads as: *I'm annoyed, I don't care, or I'm emotionally constipated but refusing to talk about it.*

The person on the other end starts spiraling: *Are they mad? Did I do something? Was that too much?* Now you've started a whole mental soap opera without saying a single mean thing, just by being short.

Fix it: If you're in a rush, just say that.

- "Yep, that works! Heading into a meeting—will respond properly later."
- "Sounds good 👍 Will catch up after work."

A little context buys you a lot of goodwill.

---

2. "K" is not an answer—it's a conversation ender

Unless you're texting from a flip phone in 2004, don't send "k." Don't send "." Don't send the thumbs-up emoji unless you *absolutely* want to sound like a disappointed dad who just got Venmo'd the wrong amount.

Tone is everything. And in texting, tone = punctuation, timing, emoji choice, and how many milliseconds it took you to type something back.

Remember: If your reply could be tattooed on someone's anxiety, re-write it.

---

3. Emojis can save or sabotage your whole point

A well-placed emoji can soften a direct message. A poorly placed one can make you look like you're mocking someone's trauma.

There's a world of difference between:

- "That was a bit intense 🙃"
- and "That was a bit intense 😬"
- and "That was a bit intense 😂"

Each one tells a different story. So, before you hit send, double-check: **Am I using this to add tone, or hide behind it?**

Also: never use the crying-laughing emoji while giving critical feedback. Unless you want your friend/client/date to block you mid-sentence.

---

4. Passive-aggressive texting is modern-day gaslighting

If you're sending a "no worries!" text while rage-blinking into your pillow, just... don't. That energy leaks through the screen like emotional smoke.

Things that sound polite but aren't:

- "No problem :)"
- "Whatever works best for you I guess."
- "Noted."
- "Sure."
- "As you wish."
- The dreaded: "." (yes, a lone period counts)

If you're mad—be honest. If you're not ready to talk—say that. If you're spiraling, step away from your phone until you're not typing like a wounded poet with a Wi-Fi connection.

Mature communication is not about being endlessly polite.

It's about **not weaponizing politeness when you're actually pissed.**

---

5. Timing matters more than grammar

The way we interpret digital messages has more to do with *when* someone replies than *what* they say.

Example:

- "I'm so sorry about what happened." (immediate) → thoughtful.
- "I'm so sorry about what happened." (after 48 hours of silence) → suspicious.

A late response doesn't always mean someone's cold or careless, but if your pattern is to go quiet when someone's vulnerable, don't be surprised if they stop coming to you.

If you're not ready to engage, it's okay to say,

"I saw this. I want to respond properly but I need a second. I'll get back to you tonight."

That's respect. That's adulting. That's how you don't become the reason someone double-texts in shame.

Try This: The Digital Tone Audit

Scroll through your last 10 texts with someone you care about. Look at your:

- word choice
- response time

- emoji tone
- punctuation habits
- where you ghosted and pretended you didn't

Ask:
If I received these messages, would I feel heard, dismissed, confused, or low-key gaslit?

Then tweak accordingly.

Texting doesn't need to be a psychological puzzle. It just needs to feel human.

Reclaim Your Power: Stop Shrinking in the Silence

That text you reread 14 times? The one where you worried you sounded too blunt, too needy, too… much?

Yeah. Let's talk about that.

Digital silence can feel brutal. You pour your heart (or at least your slightly vulnerable thought) into a message, and get hit with a "k." Or nothing at all. And suddenly you're spiraling, convinced you were too intense, too wordy, too emotional, too *everything*.

But here's the truth: **your message wasn't too much. Their response was too little.**

You don't need to shrink your expression just because someone else doesn't know how to receive it. You don't need to gut your personality to fit into a two-second read time.

Stop translating yourself into dry one-liners so you don't "scare them off." Stop editing your humanity out of your messages like it's a liability.

You're allowed to sound warm. Curious. Confident. Thoughtful. Bold. Weird.

Your voice still counts—even if it's typed. Even if it's seen and not answered.
Even if it makes someone uncomfortable.

Because if being fully expressed online means the wrong people ghost you? *Good.* That's not a loss. That's clarity.

Zoom Without the Dread

Can I just say that I hate video calls?.. with passion?

They're awkward. They're energy-draining. They force you to make intense eye contact with your own under-eye circles while pretending to care about a spreadsheet someone's screen-sharing for twenty minutes too long. Zoom fatigue is real, and it's not just about screen time—it's about the *performative exhaustion* of pretending you're 100% engaged while your soul is slipping out the window.

But here's the thing. We're not getting rid of video calls anytime soon. Whether it's a team meeting, a client check-in, or a last-minute "can we just jump on a quick Zoom?" request from someone who absolutely could have sent an email—virtual presence matters.

So, let's make it suck less, shall we?

---

1. Turn your camera on (unless there's a legit reason not to)

Nobody wants to say this out loud, so I will: if you never turn your camera on, people start to wonder why.

Yes, privacy matters. Yes, there are bad hair days and toddler meltdowns and messy apartments and weird light angles that make you look like a haunted Victorian child. But if your camera's *always* off? That reads as disengaged—even if you're fully present.

Doesn't have to be perfect lighting or full glam. Just show your face like a human. It builds trust. It signals respect. It reminds people you're more than a name in a grid.

---

2. Sit like someone might screenshot you

Look, no one expects you to be a statue of productivity. You can sip your coffee. You can lean back. But if you're slumped halfway down your chair like you're about to slip under your desk and nap, it doesn't exactly scream "I'm listening."

You don't need to be stiff or formal. But you do need to *look awake*. Bare minimum:

- Sit up.
- Nod occasionally.
- Stop staring at your second monitor like it owes you money.

---

3. Use your actual voice

One of the weirdest things about virtual meetings is how easy it is to disappear. You're there, but you're not *there*. And then someone calls your name and you scramble to unmute and say something vaguely competent while praying your voice doesn't crack like a pubescent boy on karaoke night.

Stop doing that to yourself.

Speak up *before* someone calls on you. Even just a "That makes sense" or "Good point" shows you're tracking. If you do have something to say, don't wait for a formal invitation. You're not at Hogwarts. You're at work.

And if you really want to be heard? Don't mumble through a bad mic with a ceiling fan in the background. Fix your audio. You don't need a podcast setup, just a headset and a bit of effort.

---

4. Don't multitask like a gremlin

Yes, we all do it. We check our phones. We open other tabs. We pretend to take notes while actually ordering Thai food.

But multitasking isn't subtle. People *can* tell when you're checked out—even if you've mastered the "I'm totally listening" facial expression while responding to emails. You're not fooling anyone.

If you're going to zone out, at least do it with your mic off and camera off and don't expect to be looped into the next decision. Otherwise? Stay in it. You don't need to speak every five minutes, but give signals that you're mentally here.

---

5. Shorter is better. Always.

If you're running the meeting, keep it tight. The "let's quickly sync" meeting that turns into a 50-minute existential ramble is the reason people mute themselves and scream into throw pillows.

- Start on time.
- Have a point.
- Don't recap every email from the last 72 hours.
- End early if possible—you'll be everyone's hero.

And if you're not running the meeting? Don't derail it with random side stories, tech rants, or "just one quick thing" that turns into a 10-minute monologue about last quarter's metrics. Respect the collective brain-power in the room. Everyone wants to leave.

Try This: The 3-Minute Replay Test

After your next Zoom, ask yourself:

- If someone replayed a clip of me in that meeting, would I look engaged or dead inside?
- Did I contribute clearly or ramble out loud trying to form a thought in real time?
- Did I make it easier or harder for the team to get through that hour?

You don't need to be the star of the call. But you do want to be someone people are glad was there.

Fixing Digital Miscommunication Before It Blows Up

We've all been there, yeah, me too... You send a message you *think* is neutral, and then you get the dreaded pause. No reply. Just... vibes. The tone shifts. Suddenly they're weird with you, or they send back something a little too clipped. And now you're rereading your own text like it's the Zapruder film trying to figure out where exactly it went wrong.

This is the downside of digital communication: **you don't get real-time feedback.** You don't see the raised eyebrow or the wince or the look that says "ouch" right after your message lands. You just get silence. Or worse—passive-aggressive politeness that makes you wish you could crawl through the phone and hit rewind.

So, what do you do when things get weird?

You don't over-apologize. You don't double down. You don't send seven follow-up texts trying to smooth it over.

You take a breath, own your part, and course-correct. Fast.

---

1. Acknowledge, don't grovel

You don't need a three-paragraph email or a Shakespearean apology. Most digital tension can be defused with a quick, human, one-sentence acknowledgment.

Try:

- "That didn't land how I meant it—my bad."

- "I think I could've worded that better. Let me try again."
- "Did that sound off? Wasn't my intention."

Short. Accountable. Non-dramatic.

It tells the other person you're aware, you're not defensive, and you're trying to get it right.

---

2. Don't let silence fester

If you sense something's off, don't spiral silently. You don't have to jump in immediately, but if it's been a full day and the energy still feels weird, say something.

"Hey, did I mess that up?" is better than letting the whole conversation rot in ambiguity. Most people would rather clear it up than stew in weirdness. And if they're *not* open to resolution? That's not on you. But at least you showed up like an adult.

---

3. Rephrase, don't repeat

If your message hit wrong, don't just copy-paste it with a smiley face at the end. People don't need louder—they need clearer.

Reframe the point in plain, neutral language.

Drop the sarcasm.

Lose the snark.

Say what you meant as if you were talking to a friend you respect on a day when you're not overtired and low-key cranky.

---

4. Know when to stop talking

There's a fine line between accountability and performative repair. Say what needs to be said—**once**. Then give the other person space to respond.

If you keep checking in, apologizing, clarifying, or over-explaining, it starts to feel like you're making it about your discomfort instead of their experience. That's not resolution. That's reassurance-seeking.

Let it breathe.

Try This: The Damage Control Protocol

Next time you send something that goes sideways:

1. **Pause**: Don't react to their reaction. Sit with it for an hour.
2. **Re-read**: Look at what you actually wrote. Not what you *meant*, but what it says.
3. **Check your tone**: Was it cold? Too abrupt? Weirdly intense?
4. **Send a one-sentence clarification**: That's it. No novels.
5. **Move on**: If they want to talk, they will. If they don't, take the lesson and keep it pushing.

You don't have to be perfect in digital communication. You just have to be willing to repair when things go off course. Most people don't need you to nail it every time—they just want to know you're self-aware enough to try again.

Own your words. Fix your misses. Then let them speak for themselves.

Digital communication doesn't give you tone of voice, body language, or the grace of in-person energy. All you've got are words, timing, and your ability to not text like an emotionally stunted raccoon.

But here's the good news: once you learn how to use those tools with intention, you become the kind of person people actually enjoy messaging. You get replies. You build trust. You stop accidentally starting fights with a rogue period. It's not about being a perfect texter or email wizard—it's about sounding like *you*, even through a screen.

Direct. Thoughtful. Human.

CHAPTER 7:

Storytelling That Sticks, Because Facts Are Boring AF

Stories are like duct tape—they fix everything. And if you're not using them in your communication, you're basically trying to build IKEA furniture without the instructions.

Why Stories Are Your Secret Weapon

When you hear a story, your brain doesn't just process the words—it *syncs up* with the person telling it. It's called **neural coupling**, and it means your brain starts lighting up in all the same areas as theirs. If they're talking about running through the rain barefoot, your motor cortex fires. If they're describing a warm cinnamon roll, your sensory cortex kicks in like you just took a bite. That's not imagination—that's biology. Stories make us **feel** what someone else is saying. Try doing that with a pie chart or bullet points. You can't. Because no matter how smart your stats are, if you want to connect, influence, or actually be remembered, you need to speak to the part of the brain that *feels* before it thinks. And that part speaks fluent story.

Yup, your brain is a sucker for a good story. A real one. With emotion, mess, stakes, and maybe a little chaos.

You think people are logical. Rational. Motivated by evidence. Err! You're wrong. People are messy and emotional. **People want to feel something before they decide anything.** You don't need a neuroscience degree to know this, just scroll through any group chat during a breakup. People want the *tea*, not the transcript.

And your brain? It's not reading messages like a neutral inbox. It's scanning for survival, connection, and emotional context. It wants dopamine. Oxytocin. **It wants to care.** That's why the minute you start telling a story—any story—people lean in.

Because now there's a human. A moment. A mood.

Suddenly, your message has a pulse.

You could hit someone with a perfectly reasoned argument about why they should listen to you… or you could tell them about the time you almost got fired for saying what needed to be said, and how it taught you everything you now know about boundaries. Guess which one they'll remember?

Here's the magic trick nobody talks about: **stories bypass the part of the brain that filters for BS.**

If you say, "Let me tell you why I'm right," people **brace for impact**.

If you say, "Here's something wild that happened last week," they **relax**. Their guard drops. They start tracking your *experience*, not evaluating your *stance*.

That's when persuasion happens. That's when connection happens. And that's why storytelling isn't some fluffy "soft skill" you tack onto presentations to seem engaging. It's the *core* of communication. The glue between ideas. The reason anyone gives a damn in the first place.

The best communicators in the world—whether they're CEOs, artists, salespeople, or your friend who can make a trip to the grocery store sound like an Oscar-nominated short film—they all use stories to do the heavy lifting. And it's not because they're natural-born performers. It's because they've learned what most people haven't:

Facts inform. Stories transform.

Now, let me be clear: this isn't about spinning dramatic tales for attention. It's about anchoring what you're saying in something real. Human. Specific. Because specificity is what makes people care. You don't need to tell the story of your life. Just tell the story of that one time something actually hit, changed, or clarified something for you, and say it in your own words, not like you're auditioning for a TEDx event in someone's garage.

Here's a little moment of truth for you: if you can't get someone to care about **you**, they're not going to care about your **message**. And they're definitely not going to remember it. But if you can anchor it in something they **feel**—even for 10 seconds—you've just cut through the noise. That's the holy grail of communication in 2025.

So, don't overthink it. You don't need a dramatic arc. You don't need perfect pacing. You just need to stop rattling off points like a talking Excel sheet and start talking like someone who's lived something.

People don't remember what you told them. They remember what they felt when you told it.

Storytelling in Real Life (How to Not Sound Like a TED Talk Wannabe)

Here's what most people get wrong: they either *overdo it*—full dramatic pauses, way too much backstory, pacing like they're waiting for applause—or they completely undersell it, fumbling through details with the energy of someone who's not even sure why they started talking. You don't need either extreme. You need something that feels real, casual, and emotionally sticky.

Let's break it down.

---

1. Tell stories like you're talking to one person—not the internet

You're not presenting. You're connecting. Talk like you're sharing a memory, not like you're pitching a business case to a panel of judges with no sense of humor.

Bad example:

"In 2017, I faced a major personal reckoning which led to a transformation in my understanding of self-worth..."

Better:

"Okay, so in 2017 I made a terrible decision that ended with me crying in the backseat of an Uber while trying to pretend I wasn't crying. Here's what that taught me…"

One sounds rehearsed. The other sounds like someone worth listening to.

---

2. Cut the plot summary—zoom in on *the moment*

A good story doesn't need your whole life's timeline. It needs *one vivid moment* that made something click.

Not:

"When I started that job, I didn't know what I was doing, and I was overwhelmed, and my team was struggling…"

Try:

"Two days in, my manager looked me dead in the eye and said, 'I don't care if you're new. Fix it.' And that's when I realized: confidence wasn't optional—it was expected."

Give people *a snapshot*, not a docuseries.

---

3. Make yourself the butt of the joke (sometimes)

Want to sound relatable? Don't make yourself the hero. Make yourself the *person who learned something the hard way*. The person who blew it. Who tried too hard. Who accidentally emailed the CEO instead of your coworker and had to live with that digital scar for life.

Self-deprecating humor done well is charm. Self-aggrandizing storytelling is cringe.

Let the story punch you once or twice before you punch it back with the lesson.

---

4. Tell the truth, not just the angle

You don't need to fabricate tension or inflate drama. People connect to honesty, not theater. If the story only makes sense when you embellish the stakes, it's not the right story—or you haven't found the real point yet.

Sometimes the lesson is subtle. Sometimes it's not even clear until you say it out loud. That's fine. Clarity can come in the telling. But don't fake it. It ruins the whole effect.

If your story doesn't sound like you, no one will believe the message behind it.

---

5. Anchor it to a feeling, not a fact

People don't replay facts in their head when they're trying to remember you—they replay *moments that made them feel something.*

So, when you're choosing a story to tell, ask:

- What *emotion* do I want them to feel?
- What part of this experience actually *mattered*?
- What stayed with *me*, and why?

Then say *that* part. Because if it left a mark on you, there's a good chance it will leave one on them, too.

The Sticky Story Formula

You don't need to be a "storyteller." You need to be a communicator who doesn't bore people into spiritual dissociation.

So, let's simplify the hell out of this.

You don't need character arcs. You don't need a dramatic climax. You don't need to pretend your life is a Netflix mini-series with prestige lighting and a soundtrack by Phoebe Bridgers.

You need **three things**:

1. **A moment**
2. **A feeling**
3. **A shift**

That's it. That's your story formula. Tattoo it somewhere.

---

1. The Moment

Every sticky story starts with a moment. Not a concept, not a life summary—one single, vivid *thing* that happened.

This isn't:

"I was struggling with impostor syndrome for years."

This is:

"I was in a meeting, trying to act like I belonged, and someone asked a basic question I didn't know the answer to. I laughed like it was a joke and then immediately broke out in a sweat."

That's the moment. That's the thing someone can picture. That's where your story begins.

---

2. The Feeling

Now anchor it to the emotion.

What made that moment stick wasn't what happened—it's what it meant to you. How it felt in your body. What it triggered. And if you skip this, your story will fall flat, no matter how "good" it is.

Try:

- "I felt like everyone could see through me."
- "I didn't even know where the shame was coming from. It just *flooded* me."
- "I knew I was overreacting, and I couldn't stop."

Don't tell us what happened. Tell us *what it did to you.* That's what hooks people. That's what makes it sticky.

---

3. The Shift

This is where most people either overshoot or forget the point entirely. They either launch into a full thesis on personal growth (nobody asked) or stop right after the drama like it's a reality show cliffhanger.

Your story doesn't need to be profound. But it needs a shift.

- What did you learn?
- What changed?
- What decision did it push you toward?
- What do you now see differently because of it?

It can be subtle. It can be messy. It can even be unfinished.

The goal is not to tie it up with a bow. The goal is to show that the moment *meant something.* That's what gives the story weight.

Try This: Plug It In

Here's your formula:

Moment → Feeling → Shift

Try saying it aloud. Something like:

"So there I was, sweating in a too-tight blazer, nodding like I understood everything. And I swear, the second someone looked at me, I thought I was going to melt. I realized I'd rather look like I knew nothing than ask a single question and risk sounding stupid. That moment? That's when I knew I was shrinking to be liked. I haven't done it since."

That's it. No epic tale. No fake vulnerability. Just one real, human moment with enough depth to land.

And the best part? You can use this anywhere:

- In a meeting, to make your point stick.
- In a relationship, to explain why something matters.
- On stage, if that's your thing.
- On a date, when you're tired of swapping bios and want to get real.

This formula is your shortcut to **being heard without performing**.

Use it.

Common Storytelling Mistakes (and How to Avoid Them)

The reality is, most people are *almost* good storytellers.

They've got the idea, the energy, the funny voice. But then they lose you halfway through because they took a wrong turn and now you're in a weird 8-minute detour about someone's cousin's dog and you forgot what the point even was.

So, let's fix that.

Mistake 1: Rambling Until You Forget the Point

You started off strong, but now you're five tangents deep, you've forgotten why you started, and everyone's mentally buffering like their brain is stuck on 3G.

Fix it: Practice your stories in your head *once*—not to script them, but to make sure you know where the hell you're going. One moment. One feeling. One shift. That's it.

And if you're already in too deep? **Say:**

"Wait, I just realized I'm going full audiobook here—let me get to the point."

It's charming. It works.

Mistake 2: Trying to Sound Deep Instead of Being Real

You don't need to end your story with a life lesson wrapped in a Rumi quote. People connect to *truth*, not fake depth.

Fix it: Tell the part you'd normally skip. The insecurity. The ego. The moment you made it worse. That's what makes the story relatable. If it's too polished, it reads like performance.

Mistake 3: Making Yourself the Main Character in Every Scene

Not every story has to be about you being right, brave, clever, or the only emotionally intelligent person in a world full of toddlers.

Fix it: If you're always the hero in your stories, you're probably exhausting to listen to. Try being the one who messed up, missed the cue, or had to learn the hard way. That's what builds trust. And bonus: it's way funnier.

Mistake 4: Burying the Emotion

Listing events is not storytelling. It's a calendar. And nobody bonds over your itinerary.

Fix it: Name the feeling. Own the awkward. Paint the emotional mess, not just the factual timeline. Don't just say what happened—say what *it meant.*

Mistake 5: Holding the Lesson Hostage

You're building this whole thing up, and then you end it with: "So, yeah. Anyway."

No. No no no. I mean… noooooo.

Fix it: You don't need to spell it out, but land it. Even if it's soft.

"That's when I realized I was choosing peace over honesty, and calling it maturity." "I still don't know what the right call was. But I know I won't ignore that feeling again."

The story doesn't have to solve everything. It just has to **say something.**

The Story Swap Challenge

Reading about storytelling is cute. Doing it is where the magic happens.

So, here's your no-fluff, slightly chaotic, mildly confronting challenge: **take one boring story you always tell, and swap the lens.**

Retell it using the Sticky Story Formula from earlier:

Moment → Feeling → Shift.

That's it.

Here's how it works:

Step 1: Choose a story you *always* tell

The one your friends could recite by heart. The one you default to when someone says, "Tell me about a time when…" The one you've been milking like a tired sitcom rerun.

Pick that one.

Step 2: Strip out the fluff

Ditch the long intro. Drop the scenic route through unnecessary back-story.

Cut the part where you explain what's going to happen *before* it happens.

Get straight to the **moment** that matters.

Step 3: Add the part you usually skip

The emotion. The detail. The cringe. Say the thing that made it *feel* like something, even if it wasn't dramatic. Especially if it wasn't dramatic. The magic is in the relatable.

Step 4: Land the shift

Even if it's not profound. Even if it's still a little messy.

Just name what changed.

"I realized I was performing confidence instead of building it."

"That's when I knew I wasn't just burnt out—I was invisible."

"Now I always ask the dumb question. It's never as dumb as silence."

Step 5: Try it in real life

Not on a stage. Not in a post. Just in a real conversation. At lunch. At work. In a voice note. Notice what happens.

- Do people lean in?
- Do they pause before responding?
- Do they share something deeper back?

That's the power of a good story. It creates space. It invites truth. It's not just a way to speak—it's a way to connect without begging for attention.

And if your story lands? Great. If it doesn't? Even better. That means you're *practicing*. And that means you're not just consuming this book—you're actually building the skill that makes everything else in it work.

Now go tell the damn story.

Final Thought: Stories Connect. But Pay Attention—Not Everyone's Story Is True.

By now, you've learned how to tell stories that stick—ones that make people feel something, open up, trust you. But connection goes both ways. And while storytelling is a tool for truth, it's also a tool for manipulation.

That's why the next chapter matters.

Because as much as we love vulnerability and honest communication, there's a dark side to all of it: the lies. The half-truths. The overly polished stories that sound *just a little too good.*

If you want to be a powerful communicator, you don't just need to speak well—you need to *see clearly.*

Let's activate your bullshit detector.

CHAPTER 8:

Bullshit Detector Activated: The Art of Spotting Lies

The truth is a weapon, but knowing when you're being lied to?
That's a goddamn superpower.

The Art of Spotting Lies (Without Becoming a Paranoid Wreck)

"Everybody lies."

– Dr. Gregory House, professional misanthrope and the only man who made sarcasm a diagnostic tool

And he's not wrong.

You lie. I lie. Your coworker who says they're "super excited for the team offsite" definitely lies. Most of it is harmless, social white lies, harmless ego-padding, "No really, I love your haircut" type nonsense. But sometimes? The lie is doing more than smoothing out the moment. It's covering something up. Twisting the truth. Slowly warping your sense of reality until you start questioning your own gut.

This chapter is not here to turn you into a tinfoil-hat-wearing truth hunter with an eye twitch who interrogates baristas about their weekend plans. But it *is* here to **sharpen your radar**. Because while everyone lies, not everyone's lying with the same intention, and not all lies feel the same when they hit you.

And surely, you've had moments where something felt off, but you talked yourself out of it. "Oh, they're just tired." "I'm probably being dramatic."

"They said it so calmly, it must be true."

Nope. That was your instinct getting ignored.

So now we're flipping the script. This chapter is your permission slip to pay attention to the weird stuff—the blinks, the dodges, the way their story changes slightly every time they tell it. We're not here to play detective. We're here to protect your peace.

And to be clear: *this isn't about confrontation.* It's about **discernment**. Knowing when something smells funky, even if it's sprayed with cologne. Knowing when someone's spinning a narrative, not sharing a truth.

So, grab your inner House MD. Raise an eyebrow. Let's break down what lies actually look like, and how to stop falling for them, even when they're dressed in perfect grammar and warm smiles.

The Psychology of Lying

Why do people lie?

The easy answer? Because they don't want to get caught.

The real answer is messier. Lying isn't just a moral failing—it's a social survival strategy, a panic button, a mask, a shortcut, and sometimes just a lazy Tuesday.

Think about it. Ever called in "sick" when the real illness was a desperate need to binge trash TV in peace? Ever told a friend they looked "amazing" when their outfit screamed *human highlighter with a death wish*? Or maybe you've "forgotten" to mention you're still technically married on your dating profile. Just hypothetically.

Lies aren't always malicious, but they're always intentional. And if you want to sharpen your bullshit radar, it helps to know *why* people spin stories in the first place.

The Many (Messy) Motivations Behind a Lie

Lies come in different flavors. Some are sweet. Some are bitter. Some are so toxic they leave a trail of psychological smoke damage. But every lie serves a purpose.

- **To Avoid Consequences**

  The classic "I didn't do it." Whether it's a kid with cookie crumbs on their face or a politician blaming "miscommunication," the goal is simple: dodge the fallout.

- **To Gain an Advantage**

Padding résumés, inflating sales numbers, or claiming they once met Beyoncé at Whole Foods. People lie to look better, smarter, richer, cooler.

- **To Protect Feelings**

"No, Grandma, your meatloaf isn't dry, it's... rustic." Sometimes lies are kindness in disguise. Sometimes they're just conflict avoidance with extra steps.

- **To Control the Narrative**

Manipulators lie to steer outcomes. This isn't about white lies—it's gaslighting, reality-bending, and truth-dodging as a power move.

- **To Avoid Embarrassment**

Ever nodded along in a meeting pretending to know what "blockchain integration" means? People lie to cover ignorance and save face.

- **To Fit In**

Social chameleons lie to blend. Fake jobs, fake lives, fake laughs—anything to be accepted. (Spoiler: no one's Instagram life is real.)

Reality check: Everyone lies. The difference is *why*, *how often*, and *at whose expense*.

Lying Is a Mental Workout

If you've ever told a lie and felt your brain doing somersaults—that wasn't your imagination.

Lying isn't just unethical; it's exhausting. When someone lies, their brain has to:

- **Invent a believable story** on the spot
- **Track what they've already said**
- **Watch your reactions in real time**
- **Suppress the truth while performing a fake reality**

It's like juggling flaming chainsaws while solving a Rubik's cube in your head. Eventually, something drops.

Use this to your advantage:

- Liars tend to overcomplicate—truth is usually simpler.
- They pause longer and process slower—because their brain is buffering.
- They slip up—because the mental load gets heavy fast.

Why Some People Can't Stop Lying

Then there's a different breed: the chronic liar. For them, dishonesty isn't an exception—it's the default setting.

Traits of compulsive or pathological liars:

- They lie when there's no reason to.
- They start believing their own stories.
- They lie for attention, sympathy, drama—or just because.
- They can't stop. Not because they're evil. Because they're wired for it.

Reality check: Pathological liars aren't monsters. But they *are* exhausting. You won't fix them. So, stop trying. What you *can* do is stop taking the bait.

When Lies Become Dangerous

Some lies are annoying.

Some lies unravel relationships, careers, even your sense of self. Here's where lying turns dark:

- **Gaslighting** – Rewriting reality so someone doubts their own mind.
- **Fraud** – Lies for money, power, or clout. (Fake gurus, scam artists, corporate grifters—you know the type.)
- **Betrayal** – Lies that shatter trust, especially in intimate or high-stakes relationships.
- **Compulsive deception** – People who lie so much, their whole life becomes fan fiction.

How to protect yourself:

- Trust *patterns*, not promises.
- Watch what they *do*, not what they say.
- Call out lies that *matter*. Not every lie deserves a reaction, but some? Some demand one.

Final Thought: Everyone Lies, But Not Everyone Lies the Same Way

Some lies are protective. Some are manipulative. Some are just the verbal version of cleaning up a mess you made in a panic.

Your job isn't to become a walking polygraph. Your job is to stay awake.

When someone lies, they're showing you their values—or their fear.

Either way, they're telling you something.

Now you know how to listen.

The Body Keeps the Lie

Lies don't come with neon warning signs. There's no "WARNING: FABRICATION IN PROGRESS" flashing across a liar's forehead. Instead, deception is buried in microexpressions, verbal slip-ups, and body language quirks. The trick isn't just spotting a single red flag—it's recognizing the **pattern**.

So, let's start with the body—because no matter how smooth someone is with words, the body is a terrible liar. It leaks. It glitches. It betrays even the most poker-faced fib.

And no, you don't need a psychology degree or a lie detector machine strapped to someone's chest. You just need to know what to watch for.

We're not talking about those dramatic, movie-style giveaways—no one's suddenly breaking into a sweat and looking wildly side to side like they're about to rob a bank. Real-life lies are sneakier. Subtler. Awkward in ways you might not even notice unless you're tuned in.

Here's what liars do that they *don't mean* to do:

---

1. They freeze up

You'd think liars would fidget more, but actually, the opposite is often true. When someone's fabricating on the spot, their body can stiffen. Hands disappear. Facial expressions go flat. Why? Because they're using their brainpower to manage the story, not to behave like a human.

Watch for: suddenly motionless hands, no blinking, awkwardly still posture—especially if they were animated a moment ago.

---

2. Their expressions are out of sync

Genuine emotion flows through the whole face. A real smile crinkles your eyes. A fake one? Just your mouth doing PR.

If someone says, "I'm happy for you," but their eyes look dead inside? Believe the eyes.

Bonus lie tell: expressions that show up late. If someone says "That's hilarious" *then* laughs a beat later? Their brain hit "send" before emotion arrived.

---

3. They touch their face too much

When people lie, especially under stress, they subconsciously self-soothe. That can look like rubbing the neck, scratching the nose, covering the mouth, or constantly adjusting their hair or glasses.

No, not every nose scratch is a lie. But when paired with weird tension? Your alarm bells should ding.

---

4. Their posture betrays them

Liars often do one of two things: **lean away** (subconscious withdrawal) or **suddenly square up** (overcompensating confidence).

Also, look at their feet—liars rarely think about them. Someone may be saying "Of course I'm being honest," while their feet are pointed toward the door like they're ready to moonwalk out of the conversation.

---

5. Their baseline changes

This is the golden rule: *don't compare them to other people—compare them to themselves.*

If someone's normally expressive but suddenly robotic? Red flag. If they're usually chill and now they're flustered or overselling the story with too much detail? Red flag. Lying isn't about spotting "weird" behavior—it's about a **change** in behavior.

Quick Reality Check: Anxiety ≠ Lying

Before you accuse your nervous coworker of faking the quarterly report, remember: **anxiety and deception can look similar.** Some people avoid eye contact all the time. Some people sweat when they order coffee. Don't confuse social discomfort with deception.

That's why lie detection isn't about finding *one* sign. It's about spotting a **cluster** of signals that don't match the moment—or the person.

How Liars Use Language (a Little Too Well)

Here's the fun part: the words. Because while a liar's body might betray them with awkward eye contact and rigid limbs, their **mouth** is where the real theater happens.

You might think liars trip over their words, but the really good ones? They sound *smooth. Rehearsed. Suspiciously polished.* Like they practiced in the shower and are now performing live with limited commercial interruptions.

And that's your first clue.

Because when someone's telling the truth, they don't usually care how it sounds. It's messy. Casual. A little too detailed in weird places and vague in others. That's how real stories work.

Liars, on the other hand? Their words start to smell like they were prepackaged in an anxiety lab.

Let's unpack it.

---

1. The Scripted Monologue

Liars love rehearsed-sounding lines. It's not just what they say—it's the *weird perfection* of how they say it.

"I swear, I was at home the entire night, watching Netflix. I didn't leave once. I even made popcorn."

Nobody talks like that unless they're auditioning for the role of Innocent Guy #3 in a Netflix crime doc.

What to listen for: overly complete sentences, too many details, robotic delivery. Real people pause, get interrupted, and sometimes say dumb things. Liars stick to the script.

---

2. The Detail Overdose

We've all done this. You feel like someone doesn't believe you, so you start padding your story with unnecessary fluff:

"So, I got to work at 8:47—not 8:45 because the lights at Glen Street were red, and I remember that because I saw a guy on a scooter wearing a cowboy hat and…"

Congratulations. You're spiraling.

Truth is simple. Lies need scaffolding. When someone floods you with irrelevant details, they're trying to *sound* convincing instead of just *being* convincing.

---

3. The Verbal Sanitizer

Liars often *sterilize* the language. They avoid emotional or personal words to keep it distant, clean, untouchable.

"There was an incident." "We engaged in a discussion." "I may have failed to disclose all relevant information."

Oh, you mean **you lied**, David?

Look for: overly formal, clinical language. If they sound like they swallowed a legal disclaimer, something's off.

---

4. The Repeat-and-Retreat

You ask a simple question. They respond by repeating it back to you.

"Did I take the credit card? Did I *take* the credit card?"

That's called **stalling**, friend.

Or they ask you a question instead of answering:

"Why would I do that?" "Are you seriously accusing me right now?"

Welcome to deflection city. Population: Busted.

---

5. The Morality Sales Pitch

Nothing says "I'm lying" like someone suddenly trying to convince you they're a Good Person™.

"You know I'd never do that. I've always been loyal. I believe in honesty above all."

Listen. When someone starts reading you their resume of moral virtues in the middle of a casual chat, they're not testifying—they're **covering tracks.**

---

6. The Over-Explainer

Here's the ironic part: liars talk *too much.*

Not just details. Just... *words*. Piling them on. Going off on tangents. Getting weirdly passionate about their alibi. You ask a yes-or-no question, and they give you a TED Talk.

It's called "overcompensation," and it's basically the conversational equivalent of sweating through your turtleneck in 19°C weather.

Reminder: One Lie Sign Isn't Proof

Just like with body language—*one* weird sentence doesn't mean someone's a liar. Some people ramble when they're anxious. Some people talk like a LinkedIn post because they're awkward, not deceptive.

What you're looking for is **clusters**. Patterns. A vibe that gets weirder the more you listen.

And if your gut goes, "Huh... that was too smooth," pay attention. Smooth isn't always sincere. Sometimes it's just *very practiced panic.*

Advanced Lie Detection (and "Secret" CIA Tricks That Totally Work at Dinner Parties)

Alright, you've got the basics. You know the signs. But sometimes, you want to take it one level further—not to interrogate your barista about the missing almond milk (leave the guy alone already, hasn't he suffered enough yet?), but to read people so clearly that they start watching *themselves* around you.

Here's your toolbox of advanced, borderline spy-movie tactics—minus the trench coat (unless it's your thing, of course, then go for your life), plus real-life practicality.

Yes, some of this is pulled from CIA interviewing techniques, psychological studies, and seasoned hostage negotiators. And yes, you can absolutely use them to figure out if your partner really forgot to take the bin out or just didn't want to.

---

1. Strategic Silence: Let the Lie Fill the Space

Silence makes liars sweat. Use it.

When you stay quiet after someone finishes their explanation, you're forcing them to either stand by their story—or keep talking. And the more a liar talks? The more cracks show up.

Pro move: Count to **three full seconds** after someone answers something sketchy. Nod slowly. Just… *wait.*

If they start rambling again, backpedaling, adding new "clarifications" that weren't asked for? You just watched the lie unravel in real time.

---

2. Ask the Same Question, Slightly Differently

This one's right out of the intelligence playbook. Liars rehearse **answers**, not **patterns**.

Ask a question once. Wait. Then circle back 10 minutes later and ask the same thing, just reworded. Like:

"So, what time did you say you got home again?"

then.

"Wait, were you already home by the time she called?"

If the details start shifting—times, order of events, emotional tone—it's because they're fabricating, not recalling.

---

3. Reverse the Timeline

Liars tell stories forward. Truth-tellers can jump around.

Ask for the story **backward**. Start at the end and ask them to work their way back. It disrupts any rehearsed narrative and forces the brain to re-construct, not replay.

"So, you ended up at the pub. What happened just before that?"

If they hesitate, repeat details weirdly, or get visibly irritated? That's your cue.

---

4. Watch for Emotional Mismatches

This is subtle. When people lie, their **words** and **emotions** often don't sync up. They say they're furious but smile. They say they're fine but sound defensive. They say they're confused but talk like they've rehearsed it twelve times.

The brain struggles to *fake* emotion well.

Truth? It shows up uninvited. Lies? They wear a costume, and the seams often show.

---

5. Use the Surprise Question

This one's gold. **Ask something they weren't expecting.** Something small, odd, or slightly off-topic that forces them to think *instead* of recite.

"Wait, who else was there when you said that?"

"Was it raining that night?"

They'll either pause and think (which is fine), or panic and dodge.

Liars hate improvising. They prefer their script.

---

6. Look for Passive Language and Distancing

People lying to **avoid accountability** will unconsciously avoid the word "I."

"Mistakes were made."

"There was a misunderstanding."

"Something must've gone wrong."

That's not just vague. That's **deflection by grammar**. Watch for the person disappearing from their own sentences.

---

7. Throw in a Known Truth Mid-Convo

This one's evil in the best way.

If you're not sure someone's lying, insert a known truth, but **say it like it's just another part of their story.**

"So, you left at 10, took the side street, and then the guy with the dog started yelling, right?"

If they nod along to a detail that never happened, *bingo*.

Now you're not catching the lie. You're proving the whole story is up for sale.

Final Thought: You Don't Need to Confront to Win

You don't have to yell, accuse, or throw down the truth hammer.

Most of the time, people would out themselves—you just have to give them the space, the silence, and the opportunity to talk too much.

Spotting a lie isn't about confrontation. It's about clarity.

So, when the story starts to crack?

Smile. Nod. And remember:

"Everybody lies."

But now, you're not the one being fooled.

Ethical Considerations: The Fine Line Between Skepticism and Paranoia

Knowing how to spot deception is powerful, but let's not pretend it comes without risk. Because once you **know** what to look for, it gets real easy to start side-eyeing everyone like they're hiding a burner phone and a secret second life.

But that's not the goal here.

You're not trying to become a one-person NSA. You're trying to stay awake without becoming bitter. Because when skepticism slides into paranoia? Trust breaks down. And when trust dies, so does connection.

So, let's talk about **when to call it**, when to let it slide, and how not to lose your damn mind in the process.

When to Call Out the Lie (and When to Let It Go)

Not every lie needs a courtroom-level cross-examination. Sometimes calling someone out is about as helpful as honking in a traffic jam—it makes noise, not progress.

Ask yourself:

- **What's at stake?** Is this a harmless flex or something that actually impacts you?
- **What's the intent?** Are they protecting someone's feelings—or trying to manipulate?

- **What's the endgame?** Will calling it out fix anything? Or will it just start a fight so you can win the "I knew it!" Olympics?

Reality Check: If your motivation is to be right, not to resolve—it's your ego talking, not your instincts. That's not wisdom. That's just being loud.

Over-Skepticism: When Sharp Turns Toxic

Being aware is smart. Being suspicious of *everything*? That's exhausting. For everyone.

Here's what happens when skepticism turns bitter:

- You start assuming *every* mistake is a cover-up.
- You read subtext into things that don't need decoding.
- You question praise, affection, kindness—as if people couldn't possibly mean it.

Warning signs:

- You can't take a compliment without mentally rolling your eyes.
- You second-guess close friends for no reason.
- You start trusting nobody… except some guy named "Real-Truth420" on Reddit.

That's not vigilance. That's burnout. And it leads straight to isolation.

Give People the Benefit of the Doubt

People lie, yes, but they also **mess up**. They forget. They misspeak. They phrase things weirdly. Not every inconsistency is deception. Sometimes it's just being human on a Tuesday.

Do this instead:

- Give *space* for bad memory or social awkwardness.
- Ask before accusing. "Can you clarify that?" works better than "Liar!"
- Watch for **patterns**, not one-offs. One lie? Maybe. Repeated dodges, shifting details, emotional weirdness every time something gets real? That's the one.

Lie Detection Rule #1: Don't weaponize your awareness. Use it to stay clear—not to stay cold.

Final Thought: Stay Sharp, Stay Human

Yes, you're more aware now. And yes, that awareness can save you from gaslighting, manipulation, and some grade-A workplace BS. But don't let it harden you.

You're not building walls—you're building filters.

Use your tools like this:

✓ Call out the lies that matter.

✓ Let go of the ones that don't.

✓ Ask questions before making accusations.

✓ Trust… but verify.

Because the goal isn't to become a walking lie detector. The goal is to stay safe **and** connected—to protect your peace without cutting off the world.

You don't need to be paranoid. You just need to *pay attention.*

So, you've learned how to read people. You've got the tools to spot the lies, the flinches, the verbal backflips, and the "I'm totally fine" texts that practically scream *I'm not fine at all.*

But here's the twist:

Knowing when someone's lying is only **half the power**.

The other half?

Knowing how to listen when they're telling the truth.

Because the people who *don't* lie to you—the ones who open up, get vulnerable, let their guard down—they matter. And how you listen to them? That's what builds trust, connection, and influence that doesn't need a sales pitch.

So, the next chapter?

It's not about talking. It's about shutting up, leaning in, and listening like your relationships depend on it—because they do.

Let's go.

CHAPTER 9:

Real Listening in Action (Putting Your Ears (and Ego) to Work)

Most people think they're great listeners, but here's the truth—you're probably just waiting for your turn to talk.

What Real Listening Looks Like (When It's Actually Happening)

You've read the strategies. You've seen the traps. You've probably even caught yourself mid-scroll or mid-interrupt thinking, "Shit. I do that." So, now comes the real work—not learning more tricks, but using what you already know in real time, when it matters, when your ego is twitchy, when you're tired or annoyed or trying to not say something you'll regret.

This isn't about theory anymore. It's about execution.

And speaking upfront: **most people think they're better listeners than they actually are.** They nod, they say "totally" at vaguely appropriate times, maybe they throw in a soft "I hear you" like a spiritual seasoning blend, and they call it a day. But none of that means they're actually listening. What they're doing is *performing listening*—rehearsing their next thought while waiting for a pause long enough to jump in without technically interrupting. It's the conversational version of pretending to watch a movie while actually checking your email, except worse, because someone's out here trying to feel heard and you're just mentally editing your own closing argument.

I've done this more times than I want to admit—especially when I'm three coffees deep, the other person's story has a predictable arc, and I think I know where it's going. Spoiler: I don't. Neither do you. That's the whole point of listening—you stay present long enough to be surprised. Because if you already know what someone's going to say, you're not really in the conversation. You're just building a response scaffold in your head and calling it empathy.

So, let's go there.

You're not actually listening if…

You're half-planning your reply while they're still mid-sentence. That doesn't make you prepared; it makes you unavailable. You're not absorbing—you're buffering, loading your comeback like it's a TED Talk waiting for its big moment. You're not present; you're *on deck*. And people can feel that. They always can.

You're not listening if your eyes are bouncing between their face and your phone every six seconds. You're not listening if your internal monologue is halfway through a grocery list while your mouth is busy autoplaying "uh-huh, totally, yep, makes sense." You're not listening if someone tells you something raw, and you immediately launch into your own story that's kind of similar but mostly just about you. That's not connection—that's conversational hijacking disguised as shared experience.

And maybe most importantly: you're not listening if you've already decided what they mean before they finish saying it. That's not empathy. That's assumption. And assumptions—no matter how well-intentioned—flatten people. You end up treating them like a character in a story you wrote, instead of a real human trying to hand you something true.

So. Deep breath.

Let's look at what real listening actually is.

You're listening when…

You're asking questions that aren't just fishing for validation—they're pulling for *meaning*. You're not trying to win. You're not trying to sound smart. You're not trying to guide the conversation back to your expertise or your pain or your ten-step self-help theory. You're staying curious. You're giving space. You're saying things like, *"Can you walk me through that?"* or *"What felt hard about it?"* because you genuinely want to know—not because it's your turn to speak.

You're listening when you notice the tone change. When someone says, "I'm fine," and it lands like a crack in the floor. When they pause before they hit send. When their voice drops half a register when they mention someone's name. That's listening too. It's not just about words. It's about *what they cost to say.*

And yes—this includes digital communication. Especially now, when so many conversations happen over text, chat, or DMs. If someone shares something vulnerable and your reply is "yikes" or "damn that sucks," that's not minimalism—it's dismissal wearing a hoodie. If they send a wall of text and your response is a thumbs-up emoji or a single line that starts with "lol," you've basically just told them they're a burden. You may not have meant it that way, but intent doesn't always equal impact.

Digital listening is about pacing, tone, formatting, effort. If someone types out a three-paragraph emotional dump and you hit back with "all good," congratulations—you just made them feel invisible. Even online, there are cues: delays, typos, emoji shifts. A 🙃 hits different than a 😊. You know it. We all do. So, act like it matters.

But here's the really sneaky part: **good listeners also know how to handle silence.**

Not the awkward, "I'll just fill this with small talk" silence. The kind that makes your chest feel itchy. The kind that happens when someone says something real and then... doesn't keep talking. And your instinct is to jump in with a joke, or reassurance, or something shiny to make it all feel safe again. Don't. Stay there. Let it be uncomfortable. Let them sit in the space they just created. That's where the real shit lives.

One more thing—stop trying to fix it

This might be the hardest part for people who care: realizing that fixing something isn't always the same as helping.

Someone opens up about their stress, their grief, their uncertainty, and we swoop in with a five-point plan, a TED talk we saw, a quote from Brené Brown, maybe even a phone number for a therapist. Because we want to help. We really do. But what they wanted wasn't help. What they wanted was to be witnessed.

To be *heard*, not handled.

If someone wants a solution, they'll ask. And even then, sometimes they're not asking you. They're processing. They're offering you access to something tender. And your job isn't to fix it—it's to *not flinch* when they hand it to you. Hold it carefully. Breathe. Say something like, "That makes sense," or "I'm really glad you told me that." That's listening. That's *presence*. And honestly? That's rare.

I've gotten it wrong more than I've gotten it right. I've rushed in with ideas, advice, overreaching empathy. But the moments that stuck—the ones people later told me mattered—were the ones where I said the least. Where I just stayed. Where I didn't try to move us somewhere better. I just sat in the mess with them, quietly, like that was enough. Because it was.

Listening isn't soft. It's surgical.

It's hard to stay still when everything in you wants to jump in. It's hard to hold back when you're used to being the fixer, the rescuer, the one with the right words. But if you want to change how people experience you—if you want to be the kind of person people feel *safe* around, not just impressed by—this is the work.

And no, it's not flashy. It won't get you a raise or a viral quote card or a round of applause. But you'll notice that people lean in when you speak. That they stay longer. That they trust you more. That they say things to you they don't say to anyone else. Because you *listen.*

Not perfectly.

Not always without ego.

But better than most.

And that's more than enough.

The 24-Hour Listening Challenge (Yes, You Might Hate It)

Alright, time to stop passively absorbing advice like you're binge-watching self-help for sport and *actually test your ego in the wild.* Because reading about listening is safe. It's cozy. It gives you the illusion of growth without the inconvenience of having to say, "Wow, I really don't know how to shut the hell up, do I?"

This challenge? It strips all that away.

This is **real-world, ego-bruising, brain-squirming practice**. It's designed to make you uncomfortable in the exact places you need growth. And no, it's not "hard" like summiting Everest. But it's hard in the way that requires restraint, awareness, and resisting every twitchy little impulse your nervous system has to fix, interrupt, redirect, or prove you're smart.

So. Here's what you're going to do.

Rule #1: Say less than you want to

You know that thing where someone's telling you a story and halfway through you get hit with a genius insight, or an "OMG SAME," or a full-fledged emotional TED Talk of your own? Yeah. Don't.

For the next 24 hours, commit to listening more than you talk.

That doesn't mean you have to sit there like a mute. But every time you feel the urge to jump in—pause. Breathe. Ask yourself: *Am I adding value here, or am I just adding noise?*

Most of us fill silence out of habit, not necessity. So, for one full day, let the silence breathe. Let the other person lead. Let their words hang in the air for three seconds longer than feels comfortable. That's where the gold is.

Rule #2: No fixing, solving, or "you should"-ing

This one's brutal, especially if you're the default fixer in your relationships. But here's the rule:

No unsolicited advice. No life hacks. No linking them to that podcast you swear will change everything.

If someone vents about something stressful, say, *"That sounds like a lot. Do you want to talk more about it?"* Or *"Is there something you need from me right now?"*

If they say they just want to be heard? *Believe them.* Don't assume they're passively asking for a solution in code. Don't secretly believe you know better than they do. Don't rescue them. Just *witness them.*

And if it absolutely kills you not to offer something? Write it down in your notes app. You can decide later if it's actually useful, or if it was just your inner problem-solver having a panic attack because you weren't allowed to perform usefulness for five minutes.

Rule #3: Reflect instead of react

You're not going to get this right every time. That's fine. This isn't the 24-Hour Listening Olympics. But when you catch yourself reacting—getting defensive, jumping in too fast, checking your phone while someone's mid-sentence—**stop**. Just *notice*. That's where the power is.

Try something like:

"Sorry, I realized I was already halfway into a response in my head. Can you say that last part again?"

Or:

"I noticed I felt a little defensive just now. That's on me. I'm here. Keep going."

These are small, quiet recalibrations. They make you *human*, not robotic. They show the other person that you're trying, and more importantly, that you care enough to stay in the room—even when your ego wants to make a run for it.

Rule #4: No competing for pain, struggle, or attention

This one's sneaky. Someone shares something vulnerable, and you instinctively reply with your own version of that pain—maybe worse, maybe just similar enough to shift the conversation gently (but completely) back to you.

Don't.

Your story can wait.

Let theirs breathe first.

Instead of, "I know exactly how you feel. That happened to me too—"

Try: *"That sounds really intense. I'd love to hear more if you feel like sharing."*

You're not suppressing your voice forever. You're just not making the moment about you right now. That's not silencing yourself. That's *respecting the moment.* And they will feel that.

Rule #5: No instant replies just to fill the space

This one's especially relevant in digital spaces—text, DMs, Slack, whatever. **If someone shares something meaningful, pause.** Think before you type. Give yourself three extra seconds.

Fast replies aren't always a sign of engagement. Sometimes they're a reflex. A habit. A way to get the emotional baton out of your hands so you can breathe again.

For 24 hours, practice **intentional responses**. Even if it's just:

"Thanks for sharing that with me. I'm sitting with it."

It tells the other person: *I'm here. I'm listening. And I don't need to rush this.*

What to expect (a.k.a. withdrawal symptoms)

You will probably hate it.

You will definitely get it wrong.

You will catch yourself interrupting, explaining, solving, reacting.

You'll notice how hard it is to *not* make it about you.

And you'll feel twitchy and awkward and maybe a little exposed.

Perfect.

That's the part where it's working.

Because every moment you *notice* yourself slipping back into old habits is a moment you've interrupted the automatic loop. And that's how change begins—not in a flawless performance, but in the clumsy, messy middle where you're trying something new and it feels weird as hell.

Optional journal prompt (if you're into that kind of thing)

At the end of the 24 hours, ask yourself:

- What did I learn about how I listen?
- When did I feel most tempted to interrupt or redirect?
- What shifted in how people responded to me?
- Did I feel more connected, or more distant?

No pressure. No gold stars. Just reflection.

And maybe a quiet moment where you realize how much you've been missing—not because you didn't care, but because you didn't know how to stop talking long enough to hear what was actually being said.

Now you do.

Your Listening Ego Survival Kit

I know, listening sounds easy… all the way until your **ego** shows up. And it always does. It walks into every conversation with a checklist—prove you're smart, don't look weak, don't lose control, make sure you say something impressive, stay one step ahead. And while it's doing all that mental gymnastics in the background, you're supposed to just... listen?

Yeah. Good luck with that.

And no, you're not a narcissist. You're simply a human. And humans, by default, are wired to protect the self. That means we listen for openings, for threats, for validation, for places to jump in with our story and say "me too" or "but wait" or "here's what I think." The ego doesn't mean to hijack every conversation. It just doesn't like being left out.

So, this section isn't about crushing your ego. It's about recognizing when it's **running the show**, and knowing how to gently, consistently tell it to calm the hell down.

Here's how.

Step one. Notice your defensiveness.

You know that spike you feel when someone gives you feedback? That tiny lurch in your chest when a friend says, "Hey, can I be honest with you?" That tightness in your jaw when someone disagrees with your idea? That's not clarity. That's **ego panic**. And it's usually the moment you stop listening.

Instead of reacting, try naming it. Not to the other person—unless you're feeling brave, but to yourself.

Say: I'm feeling attacked, but I'm not actually under attack.

Or: This makes me uncomfortable, but that doesn't mean it's wrong.

The goal isn't to erase the feeling. The goal is to recognize it for what it is: your ego, flailing in the corner, trying to protect your image.

You're not going to die if someone thinks you're wrong. You'll survive it. You might even learn something.

Step two. Stop listening for a gap to jump into.

If you're sitting there waiting for the conversation to hand you a spotlight, you're not listening. You're hovering. You're on deck. You're mentally crafting a quote-worthy response instead of **actually absorbing** what's being said.

Every time you catch yourself thinking, "Ooh, I've got the perfect thing to say," pause. Breathe. Ask yourself, Do I need to say this? Or do I just want to feel important?

You'd be amazed how often it's the second one.

Try this instead: Let the conversation unfold without you steering it. Ask a question you don't already know the answer to. Let the other person finish their entire thought—even if it's slow, messy, or doesn't lead anywhere profound. Listening isn't about efficiency. It's about **presence.**

Step three. Let go of the need to win.

This one stings. A lot of people confuse listening with quietly preparing their counterargument. Especially in relationships. Especially at work. You're not really hearing the other person—you're fact-checking them in real time, pulling up your receipts, scanning for weak spots in their logic so you can deliver your closing statement and walk away the perceived winner.

But here's the thing: conversations aren't courtrooms. You're not on trial. You don't get points for scoring a rhetorical touchdown while the other person is trying to explain how they feel.

So, next time you catch yourself gearing up to win the moment, ask: **What am I trying to prove here?** And who am I trying to prove it to?

If the answer is "I want to feel right," then congratulations—you've found your ego in the wild. Now breathe. Step back. Ask yourself if connection matters more than domination.

Umm.. spoiler: It does.

Step four. Don't pretend curiosity—actually be curious.

You know that thing where someone's saying something you completely disagree with, and you nod politely while silently planning your rebuttal? Yeah. That's not open-mindedness. That's ego theatre.

Curiosity doesn't mean agreeing with everything. It means staying **interested**, even when you don't. It means asking, "What made you feel that way?" instead of, "How could you possibly believe that?" It means seeing the other person as complex and layered, not a stereotype you've mentally filed under wrong, irrational, or exhausting.

If you can stay curious while being uncomfortable, you're already ahead of most people. And your conversations will go deeper than they ever have before.

Step five. Know when your ego needs a nap.

Sometimes, you're just not in the place to listen well. You're tired, stressed, emotionally fried, or two seconds away from crying in a bathroom stall. That's not a failure. That's a signal.

When your capacity is shot, the most honest thing you can do is say, "I want to give you my full attention, but I don't have it right now. Can we talk a little later when I can really show up?"

That's not selfish. That's respect—for both of you.

Listening takes energy. It takes presence. It takes being able to temporarily step out of your own storyline ,someone else can walk you through theirs. And if you don't have that to give today? That's okay. Don't fake it. Don't force it. Just own it.

The people who matter will understand.

And if they don't? Then maybe they're the ones who need this book.

Reclaim Your Power: You've Earned the Mic, Now Don't Waste It

Look at you. Sitting through awkward silences. Not steamrolling people mid-sentence. Listening without plotting your next "brilliant" one-liner.

You didn't die. You didn't explode.

And shockingly? People probably opened up more.

That's the power of real listening—it makes your words *land harder* when you finally do speak. So, now that your ego has had a forced timeout and your inner fixer is sedated, here's your next move:

When you speak, make it count.

No fluff. No rambling. No awkward detours to make sure *everyone* is comfortable. You've earned the mic—stop handing it right back like it's too hot to hold.

And if someone's wondering why you suddenly sound more grounded, more confident, more damn compelling?

Tell them this:

You stopped talking just to talk.

You started listening to understand.

And now, when you speak?

People actually shut up and listen.

Last Words Before You Open Your Mouth

If you've made it this far, you already know listening isn't a soft skill. It's a razor-sharp tool that only works if you're willing to stop swinging it around like a sword and start using it like a scalpel. It's not passive. It's not decorative. It's not the thing you sprinkle on top of a conversation to make it polite.

It's the thing that makes connection real—or not at all.

The truth is, you're going to forget all of this sometimes. You're going to interrupt. You're going to default to fixing, performing, reacting, telling your story because it's right there on the tip of your tongue and goddamn it's good. You're going to talk too soon, too loud, or not at all when someone really needed you to show up.

And that's okay. You don't have to be perfect. You just have to care enough to notice, and start again.

Every pause you hold.

Every assumption you question.

Every time you sit still in someone else's truth without sprinting to your own — That's a win.

Not because it gets you praise.

Not because it makes you sound wise.

But because it's the kind of presence that actually changes people. Including you.

So, next time you're in a conversation, ask yourself—not just, *"What do I want to say?"*

Ask: *"What do they need me to hear?"*

Start there.

Let everything else follow.

CONCLUSION:

Master the Art of Shutting Up — and Watch Everything Shift

Let's not overcomplicate this.

Everything you want—better relationships, more respect, deeper connection, actual influence—starts with one skill most people wildly overestimate in themselves: **listening**.

And throughout this book, we've ripped the fluff off that concept. You've learned how to stop over-explaining, how to walk into a room without needing to fill it with noise, how to read body language like a seasoned interrogator, and—most importantly—how to shut the hell up and actually hear what someone's trying to say.

The pattern? It was never really about what you say.

It was about how you show up.

And how you listen.

Think about the people who hold the most power in any room. It's not the loudest voice or the one spitting the most facts. It's the person who listens so well that other people feel smarter just talking to them. That's presence. That's leadership. That's the shift you're stepping into now.

Your Final Challenge: The 7-Day Listening Upgrade

Reading about listening is adorable. Doing it in real life—where people test your patience, push your buttons, and interrupt you mid-sentence—is the real flex.

So, here it is. Your 7-day crash course in **actually being that person** people want to open up to:

Day 1: In every conversation, pause three seconds before you speak. No exceptions.

Day 2: Use "Tell me more about that" at least five times, and mean it.

Day 3: Notice how often you interrupt. Then cut it in half.

Day 4: Catch yourself rehearsing a reply while someone else is talking. Stop. Refocus.

Day 5: In one difficult conversation, validate their perspective before offering yours.

Day 6: Use body language mirroring to make someone feel fully seen.

Day 7: Reflect. Did people open up more? Did things shift? Did *you*?

Do this challenge honestly and your interactions won't just feel different. They'll be **transformed**. People will lean in more. You'll stop walking away from conversations thinking, *Why didn't I say that better?* And most importantly, you'll start getting what you actually want out of your connections—clarity, trust, respect, influence, peace.

Final Thought: The World Doesn't Need Louder Voices—It Needs Better Listeners

You're surrounded by people who are desperate to feel seen.

They won't always say it, but they're hoping someone—anyone—will actually hear them without judgment, ego, or the compulsion to fix everything.

Be that person.

Be the one they remember. The one they open up to. The one they trust with the messy middle instead of the polished headline.

You don't have to master every communication technique in existence. You just have to listen better than most. That alone will change your relationships, your reputation, your entire life.

So, go do it.

Start small.

Stay curious.

Shut up when it matters.

...and watch your whole world change.

You Made It — Now Let's Talk About the Load You're Still Carrying

If you've made it this far, chances are you've started doing the real work: using your voice, setting boundaries, no longer being everyone's emotional sponge. But maybe, just maybe—there's one person still draining you. Quietly. Consistently. Maybe you're still carrying someone through their own life, while yours gets heavier by the day.

If you've done the work to be heard but **you're still doing the emotional labor in a relationship that feels like a part-time job**, then you're ready for what's next.

Book 3: You're Not His Therapist is your **no-BS survival guide** for women stuck in relationships with men who treat maturity like an optional subscription plan and emotional support like your unpaid job.

This is for you if you're tired of:

- Managing his moods like a weather system.
- Explaining your needs like a customer support agent.
- Feeling like you're parenting someone with facial hair.

You don't need more tools to communicate better.

You need tools to **stop over-functioning for someone who refuses to grow**.

Scan the QR code on the next page to join the waitlist.

Get the support. Get the strategy. Get your damn self back.

Because **you're not his therapist. You never were.**

Before You Go… A Small Ask That Makes a Massive Difference

If you've made it to the end of this book, I already know three things about you:

1. You care about becoming a better communicator.
2. You're willing to do the uncomfortable work most adults avoid.
3. You're exactly the kind of person whose voice *should* be heard more often.

So, here's your last little mission — the part where you get to help someone else who's standing right where you were when you picked this up:

Scan this code and leave an honest review.

It doesn't need to be poetic. It doesn't need to be long.

It can be as simple as:

- "I finally understand why people weren't hearing me."
- "I stopped overtalking, overthinking, and getting steamrolled."
- "This book made me communicate like an actual grown-up."

Your review helps other readers decide whether this book is worth their time, their money, and their emotional bandwidth. And for an indie author? Reviews are oxygen. They help this work reach the humans who need it most.

So, if the tools in these pages helped you speak more clearly, draw stronger boundaries, spot manipulation, or just breathe easier in conversations — **please take 30 seconds to say so.**

It matters.

More than you know.

Curious What Else I Wrote?

Turns out one book doesn't fix a whole life. (Believe me, I tried.)

Scan the second QR code to see the rest of the collection. Same voice. Same no-BS approach. Different flavours of the same underlying idea: you're not broken, you've just been handed bad advice by people trying to sell you something shinier than the truth.

Whatever's chewing on you right now — a relationship that's turned into unpaid emotional labour, money that disappears before you understand where it went, a brain that won't stop rehearsing arguments at 2am, or (yes) a garden bed that refuses to grow anything but weeds — there's probably a book for it.

Pick the one that hits closest.

No spam. No motivational speeches at 6 a.m. Just books, occasional updates, and the kind of tools your therapist would give you if she wasn't watching the clock.

And One Last Thing...

If any of this landed — if you saw yourself in the overexplainer, the overthinker, the one carrying the emotional weight of every room she walks into — there's a book you probably need more than this one.

You're Not His Therapist.

For women who keep ending up as the translator, the peacekeeper, the one running the whole conversation while he grunts at his phone.

Same voice. Same no-BS toolkit. Different problem, same underlying pattern of doing all the heavy lifting in a relationship you didn't sign up to run.

If Communication Skills gave you the words, *You're Not His Therapist* tells you when to stop wasting them on someone who isn't listening.

Scan to grab a copy. Or don't.

Actually, One More Thing

You didn't just finish a book, you rewired a skill that will change every relationship you have with another human being.

That's not small.

That's not accidental.

That's power.

Use it well.

Speak clearly.

Listen fully.

Hold your boundaries like they matter, because they do.

And never forget: **your voice deserves the room it takes up.**

References

Ames, D. R., & Wazlawek, A. S. (2014). Pushing in the dark: Causes and consequences of limited information in negotiation. *Personality and Social Psychology Bulletin, 40*(6), 775–790.

Burgoon, J. K., Guerrero, L. K., & Floyd, K. (2016). *Nonverbal communication* (2nd ed.). Routledge.

Byron, K. (2008). Carrying too heavy a load? The communication and miscommunication of emotion by email. *Academy of Management Review, 33*(2), 309–327.

Cuddy, A. J. C., Kohut, M., & Neffinger, J. (2013). Connect, then lead. *Harvard Business Review, 91*(7–8), 54–61.

Ekman, P. (2009). *Telling lies: Clues to deceit in the marketplace, politics, and marriage* (4th ed.). W. W. Norton & Company.

Ekman, P., & Friesen, W. V. (1969). Nonverbal leakage and clues to deception. *Psychiatry, 32*(1), 88–106.

Goldstein, N. J., Vezich, I. S., & Shapiro, J. R. (2014). Building rapport through mimicry: The role of high self-monitoring. *Journal of Nonverbal Behavior, 38*, 333–347.

Gottman, J. M. (1994). *What predicts divorce? The relationship between marital processes and marital outcomes.* Lawrence Erlbaum Associates.

Green, M. C., & Brock, T. C. (2000). The role of transportation in the persuasiveness of public narratives. *Journal of Personality and Social Psychology, 79*(5), 701–721.

Hasson, U., Ghazanfar, A. A., Galantucci, B., Garrod, S., & Keysers, C. (2012). Brain-to-brain coupling: A mechanism for creating and sharing a social world. *Trends in Cognitive Sciences, 16*(2), 114–121.

Hogg, M. A. (2016). Social identity theory. In S. McKeown, R. Haji, & N. Ferguson (Eds.), *Understanding peace and conflict through social identity theory* (pp. 3–17). Springer.

Kahneman, D. (2011). *Thinking, fast and slow.* Farrar, Straus and Giroux.

Knapp, M. L., Hall, J. A., & Horgan, T. G. (2014). *Nonverbal communication in human interaction* (8th ed.). Cengage Learning.

Kreps, S., & Kriner, D. (2020). The use of social media in crisis communication. *Political Science Research and Methods, 8*(1), 28–44.

Levine, T. R. (2014). Truth-default theory: A theory of human deception and deception detection. *Journal of Language and Social Psychology, 33*(4), 378–392.

Linehan, M. M. (2015). *DBT skills training manual* (2nd ed.). Guilford Press.

Mehrabian, A. (1971). *Silent messages.* Wadsworth.

Porter, S., & ten Brinke, L. (2008). Reading between the lies: Identifying concealed and falsified emotions in universal facial expressions. *Psychological Science, 19*(5), 508–514.

Rogers, C. R., & Farson, R. E. (1957). Active listening. *Industrial Relations Center of the University of Chicago.*

Stephens, N., & Koenig, A. (2019). The psychology of conversation: Interpersonal communication and the social mind. *Current Opinion in Psychology, 30*, 27–31.

Sweller, J. (1988). Cognitive load during problem solving: Effects on learning. *Cognitive Science, 12*(2), 257–285.

Tannen, D. (1995). *Gender and discourse.* Oxford University Press.

Vrij, A. (2008). *Detecting lies and deceit: Pitfalls and opportunities* (2nd ed.). Wiley.

Walther, J. B. (2011). Theories of computer-mediated communication. In M. L. Knapp & J. A. Daly (Eds.), *The SAGE handbook of interpersonal communication* (pp. 443–479). SAGE.

Zuckerman, M., DePaulo, B. M., & Rosenthal, R. (1981). Verbal and nonverbal communication of deception. *Advances in Experimental Social Psychology, 14*, 1–59.

www.ingramcontent.com/pod-product-compliance
Lightning Source LLC
LaVergne TN
LVHW022206200926
848481LV00006B/1865